The HEALTHY SWAPS Cookbook

The HEALTHY SWAPS Cookbook

Easy Substitutions to Boost
the Nutritional Value of Your Favorite Recipes

DANIELLE DAVIS
creator of Danilicious Dishes

PAGE STREET
PUBLISHING CO.

PAGE STREET
PUBLISHING CO.

First published in 2021 by

Page Street Publishing Co.

27 Congress Street, Suite 105

Salem, MA 01970

www.pagestreetpublishing.com

Distributed by Macmillan, sales in Canada by The Canadian Manda Group.

25   24   23   22   21   1   2   3   4   5

ISBN-13: 978-1-64567-247-0

ISBN-10: 1-64567-247-6

Library of Congress Control Number: 2020944075

Cover and book design by Ashley Tenn for Page Street Publishing Co.

Photography by Danielle Davis

Printed and bound in the United States of America

To my husband, Deano,

WHO ENCOURAGED ME TO START A FOOD BLOG.
WITHOUT YOU, NONE OF THIS WOULD BE POSSIBLE.

Contents

THE HEALTHY CARB MAGIC OF VEGGIES AND WHOLE GRAINS 85

LIGHTER DAIRY DISHES AND DESSERTS 115

REFINED SUGAR–FREE EATS AND TREATS 131

BRIGHT AND LIGHT LIBATIONS 151

INTRODUCTION

My main goal for this cookbook was to create approachable, crave-worthy recipes using real, wholesome and nutritious ingredients.

Here's the thing about healthy eating: Many people overcomplicate it and make certain foods taboo. They associate healthy eating with bland, boring foods. But healthy eating and flavor are not mutually exclusive. You don't have to give up the foods you love when trying to eat better. All it takes is a few simple swaps.

This cookbook will show you how to enjoy your favorite foods in a healthier way simply by using the right ingredients.

In each chapter of this cookbook, I'll introduce you to new swap ingredients based on different categories: proteins, flours, fats, carbs, dairy, sugars and drinks. These swap ingredients aim to amp up the health benefits in your meals by adding elements such as fiber, protein and vitamins while also lowering the sugar and fat content and maintaining the integrity and flavors of your favorite foods.

Just what will you find in these pages?

In Lean and Clean Mains (page 13), I'll show you how to lighten up your favorite main dishes using lean, nutritious proteins and vibrant, fresh ingredients to make meals like Smoky Turkey Chili (page 20), Slow-Cooker Tacos al Pastor (page 17) and Healthy Chicken Parmesan (page 35).

Alternative Flours—Have Your Cake and Eat It Too! (page 41) will introduce you to alternative, nutrient-rich flours that replace starchy white flour. If you're in the mood for something sweet, try my Gluten-Free Chocolate and Citrus Olive Oil Cake (page 53). Or, to satisfy that craving for something savory, make the Almond Flour Chicken Tenders (page 45).

Next, Spectacular Suppers and Snacks Using Healthy Fats (page 57) will show you how to replace heavy ingredients like butter and mayo with nutrient-dense ingredients like Greek yogurt and coconut oil to re-create some of your favorite dishes. You'll love my lightened-up Greek Yogurt Beef Stroganoff (page 58) paired with the Healthier New York–Style Cheesecake with Macerated Strawberries (page 79) for a company-worthy supper. Or, if you're in a hurry for lunch, you can whip up the Cobb Salad with Avocado Ranch (page 62) with a side of Caramelized Onion Dip with Roasted Veggie Chips (page 70) for a healthy midday meal.

In The Healthy Carb Magic of Veggies and Whole Grains (page 85), I will show you how to create flavor-packed and filling meals through some unique uses of veggies and nutritious grains, such as quinoa and farro. The result: dishes like my Steak Fajita Brown Rice Bowls (page 105) and Korean Barbecue Cauliflower Wings (page 90).

In the chapter entitled Lighter Dairy Dishes and Desserts (page 115), I'll show you alternatives to fatty dairy products that will lighten up your pasta and ice cream treats, like my Creamy Cashew Alfredo (page 120) and Strawberry-Banana Nice Cream (page 127).

Refined Sugar–Free Eats and Treats (page 131) will show you how to use products like honey, maple syrup and coconut sugar—which are easier on digestion but just as tasty as white sugar—to make your favorite baked goods and savory dishes. Whether you need something healthy for dinner—like Honey-Dijon and Pecan Baked Salmon (page 141)—or a delicious low-sugar treat for that family get-together—like Grandma's Texas Sheet Cake (page 146)—you'll find dishes that are tasty and better for you in this chapter.

Finally, I even lighten up cocktails in Bright and Light Libations (page 151). In the warmer months, sit back and relax with some Citrus Rosé Sangria (page 155), and when the weather gets chilly and gray, warm yourself with a mug of Bourbon-Maple Hot Chocolate (page 160)—because we all need a good drink now and again!

This cookbook is not about following any particular diet or banning certain foods. Dieting rules feel restrictive and cumbersome, and they tend to make cooking stressful and eating unenjoyable. That's wrong! That's why this cookbook focuses on finding ways to make every meal healthier by incorporating simple swaps. Some recipes are limited to one swap, while others incorporate multiple swaps. In some recipes, I still use real butter or sugar but replace the flour or dairy to lighten up the dish. Sometimes a recipe will be gluten-free or vegan-friendly, while other times the recipe is not particular to any diet. Whatever the swap, the goal is always the same: to make good food that's good for you.

Slight adjustments to your favorite foods will allow you to eat healthier on a sustainable basis. Through some simple swaps, this book shows you just how to do it.

Let's get to cooking!

XOXO,
Danielle

Danielle Davis

LEAN *and* CLEAN MAINS

The Swap: Lean proteins instead of high-fat, calorie-dense meats.

....

When I was growing up, my mom made dinner for us every night. Eating home-cooked meals as a family was a sacred tradition that we did Monday through Friday. My parents, three brothers and I would share stories from our days as we enjoyed a delicious meal together. My mom is an amazing cook, and some of my favorite meals were tacos, spaghetti and meatballs, chili and chicken tenders.

These meals, though comforting and nostalgic, weren't always the healthiest. As was the custom in the '90s, my mom used full-fat and sometimes processed ingredients to aid in her cooking. For instance, for taco night, she used fatty ground beef and packaged, processed taco seasoning.

As an adult, I keep the tradition of sitting down and eating dinner with my family every weeknight alive. I also still eat the meals I loved as a kid. The only difference is that I make these meals much healthier by incorporating a few simple swaps, particularly by using healthier, leaner proteins to make my favorite meals nutritious too.

In this chapter, I will show you how to make delicious and healthy main dishes using cleaner proteins and less-processed ingredients to make every dish shine. Taco night is still a staple in my house, but I use leaner pork, slowly cooked to perfection in a smoky homemade pineapple marinade and served with a fresh pineapple salsa, to make Slow-Cooker Tacos al Pastor (page 17). For cool fall evenings, I make a very comforting and hearty, but much more nutritious Smoky Turkey Chili (page 20). I also still enjoy a healthy version of a nostalgic comfort dish, Spicy Buttermilk Ranch "Fried" Chicken (page 30). There are also dishes inspired by cuisines from around the world to help liven up family dinners, like my Jamaican Jerk Grilled Chicken Wraps (page 33) and Chicken Shawarma and Quinoa Bowls (page 25).

These nutritious and flavor-packed meals are sure to keep your loved ones full and healthy while making family dinners memorable too.

THAI TURKEY MEATBALLS

Ground turkey is a great alternative to beef because it's low in fat and high in protein. Turkey gets a bad rap for lacking flavor, but these Thai Turkey Meatballs are anything but boring. They're tender, juicy and bursting with big flavors from fresh herbs and spices like garlic and ginger. The meatballs soak up a spicy and creamy coconut curry peanut sauce. It's all served over a bed of warm, fluffy brown basmati rice. It's the perfect combination of cozy and healthy. This delicious and satisfying dish will turn you into a ground turkey lover!

YIELD: 4 TO 6 SERVINGS

Thai Turkey Meatballs

1 lb (454 g) lean ground turkey

1 large egg, beaten

½ cup (45 g) whole-wheat panko breadcrumbs

1 tbsp (15 ml) soy sauce

1 to 2 tsp (5 to 10 ml) Sriracha

¾ tsp salt

¼ tsp black pepper

¼ cup (25 g) coarsely chopped green onion

¼ cup (12 g) coarsely chopped fresh cilantro

¼ cup (35 g) coarsely chopped water chestnuts

2 tsp (6 g) minced ginger

2 tsp (6 g) minced garlic

To make the Thai turkey meatballs, combine the turkey, egg, breadcrumbs, soy sauce, Sriracha, salt, black pepper, green onion, cilantro, water chestnuts, ginger and garlic in a large bowl. Gently mix until the ingredients are thoroughly incorporated; do not overmix the ingredients. Allow the mixture to rest for 5 minutes.

Meanwhile, grease a large baking sheet or line it with parchment paper.

Using a cookie scoop or small spoon, scoop out portions of the turkey mixture and roll each into a ball. You should be able to create 16 to 18 medium-sized meatballs.

Place the meatballs on the prepared baking sheet. Place the baking sheet in the refrigerator for 1 hour to allow the meatballs to firm up. Remove the baking sheet from the refrigerator 15 minutes before baking the meatballs.

Preheat the oven to 400°F (204°C). Bake the meatballs for 16 minutes, flipping them halfway through the baking time, until the meatballs are light golden brown.

(Continued)

Coconut Curry Peanut Sauce

1 tbsp (15 ml) extra virgin olive oil or sesame oil

½ medium white onion, thinly sliced

1 medium red bell pepper, thinly sliced

¾ to 1 tsp salt, divided

1 tbsp (9 g) minced garlic

1 tbsp (9 g) minced ginger

2 tbsp (30 g) red curry paste

1 (15-oz [444-ml]) can light or full-fat coconut milk

¼ cup (65 g) smooth peanut butter

3 tbsp (45 ml) honey or agave

2 tbsp (30 ml) fish sauce

2 tbsp (30 ml) soy sauce

½ tbsp (8 ml) rice wine vinegar

½ tbsp (5 g) cornstarch

1 tbsp (15 ml) cold water

Juice of ½ small lime

For Serving

2 cups (370 g) brown basmati rice, cooked

½ cup (24 g) finely chopped fresh cilantro

Meanwhile, make the coconut curry peanut sauce. Heat the oil in a large skillet over medium heat. Add the onion, bell pepper and ½ teaspoon of the salt and cook the mixture for 2 to 4 minutes, until the onion is translucent. Add the garlic and ginger and cook the mixture for 1 to 2 minutes, until the garlic and ginger are fragrant. Add the red curry paste and cook it for about 2 minutes, until it becomes a rusty red color.

Add the coconut milk, peanut butter, honey, fish sauce, soy sauce, vinegar and remaining ¼ to ½ teaspoon of salt and stir until the ingredients are well incorporated. Bring the sauce to a low boil and cook it for 3 to 5 minutes, until it thickens slightly.

Combine the cornstarch and cold water in a small bowl and mix them together until no lumps are present. Add the cornstarch slurry to the sauce and stir to combine it with the sauce. Increase the temperature to medium-high and cook the sauce for 3 to 5 minutes, until it thickens slightly.

Taste the sauce and adjust the seasonings as necessary. Add the lime juice and stir it into the sauce.

Reduce the heat to medium-low and bring the sauce to a gentle simmer. Add the meatballs and cook them in the sauce for 3 to 5 minutes, until the meatballs' internal temperature reads 165°F (74°C) and they have absorbed the sauce.

To serve, place the meatballs over the rice and garnish the meatballs with the cilantro.

Note: These meatballs go great with my spiced cashews (page 123).

Extra Swaps: The sauce is sweetened with only honey, so it's free of refined sugar. I also use coconut milk to make this a dairy-free dish. Finally, I serve the meatballs with brown rice to add fiber.

SLOW-COOKER TACOS AL PASTOR

Tacos al pastor is hands down my favorite taco. I was first introduced to it at our neighborhood taco joint when we lived in Chicago, and I quickly fell in love. Tacos al pastor contain slowly roasted and super-flavorful pork paired with juicy, sweet pineapple. To re-create this taco for a delicious, healthy weeknight dinner, I use a pork shoulder roast and trim most of the fat to make it much leaner. It's still scrumptious and juicy, thanks to a delicious marinade and a slow cooker. Roasting the onions and pineapple is the secret to bringing out their natural sweetness and imparting a smoky flavor to the marinade. The marinade also includes bold flavors like adobo, cumin, garlic and bright notes of citrus. This taco is just as good, if not better, than the one I fell in love with in Chicago!

YIELD: 12 TO 15 TACOS

....

Tacos

3½ lb (1.6 kg) pork shoulder roast, bone-in or boneless, trimmed of excess fat

3½ tsp (19 g) salt, divided

1½ tsp (3 g) black pepper

1 small onion, coarsely chopped

2 cups (330 g) coarsely chopped fresh pineapple

2 tbsp (30 ml) avocado oil or extra virgin olive oil, divided

2½ tbsp (23 g) brown sugar or coconut sugar

2 tbsp (30 ml) fresh lime juice

1 tbsp (6 g) lime zest

3 tbsp (45 ml) fresh orange juice

1 tbsp (6 g) orange zest

¼ cup (60 ml) chicken broth

2 tbsp (30 ml) apple cider vinegar

4 to 5 cloves garlic

2 to 3 chipotle peppers in adobo sauce

1 tsp adobo sauce

2 tbsp (18 g) chili powder

1 tsp ground cumin

1 tsp ground coriander

1 tsp dried oregano

½ tsp onion powder

¼ tsp ground allspice

12 to 15 (6" [15-cm]) corn tortillas

To make the tacos, preheat the oven to 400°F (204°C). Grease a large baking sheet.

Season the pork with 3 teaspoons (15 g) of the salt and the black pepper, making sure to cover the whole pork shoulder. Set the pork aside.

Place the onion and pineapple on the prepared baking sheet. Drizzle the onion and pineapple with 1 tablespoon (15 ml) of the oil and sprinkle them with ¼ teaspoon of the salt. Roast the onion and pineapple for 16 to 18 minutes, flipping them halfway through the cooking time, until the onion and pineapple are tender. Add the brown sugar and toss the roasted onion and pineapple to coat them. Roast the onion and pineapple for 2 to 3 minutes, until they start to caramelize.

Transfer the onion and pineapple to a blender. Add the lime juice, lime zest, orange juice, orange zest, remaining 1 tablespoon (15 ml) of oil, broth, vinegar, garlic, chipotle peppers, adobo sauce, chili powder, cumin, coriander, oregano, onion powder, allspice and remaining ¼ teaspoon of salt. Blend the ingredients until a smooth, thick sauce forms.

Place the pork in the slow cooker. Cover the pork in the pineapple sauce. Cook the pork on low heat for 8 hours.

Take the pork out of the slow cooker. Remove the bone if you are cooking a bone-in pork shoulder. Remove any fatty pieces, then shred the pork using forks or tongs. Transfer the pork to a large serving bowl and add ½ cup (120 ml) or more of the leftover sauce from the slow cooker, if desired.

(Continued)

Pineapple-Avocado Salsa

½ small red onion, diced

1½ cups (248 g) diced fresh pineapple

1 large avocado, diced

1 tbsp (15 ml) avocado oil

1 tbsp (15 ml) fresh lime juice

Splash of agave

2 tbsp (6 g) coarsely chopped fresh cilantro

½ tsp salt

Chipotle Mayo

⅓ cup (73 g) olive oil mayo

⅓ cup (95 g) plain Greek yogurt

2 tsp (10 ml) adobo sauce

1 tbsp (15 ml) fresh lime juice

To make the pineapple-avocado salsa, combine the onion, pineapple and avocado in a medium bowl. Add the oil, lime juice, agave, cilantro and salt and stir until all of the ingredients are well combined.

To make the chipotle mayo, combine the mayo, yogurt, adobo sauce and lime juice in a small bowl. Stir until the ingredients are well combined.

Over a gas burner or in a medium skillet over medium-high heat, slightly char the corn tortillas. Top each tortilla with the pork, pineapple-avocado salsa and chipotle mayo.

Note: If you would like to brown the seasoned pork before cooking it, heat ½ tablespoon (8 ml) of extra virgin olive oil in a large skillet or in the slow cooker's insert if your slow cooker has a sauté function. Brown the pork shoulder on all four sides for 3 to 4 minutes a side, then continue with the recipe as written.

SMOKY TURKEY CHILI

There is just something so comforting about a bowl of home-cooked chili. It's like a big, warm hug on a cold day. Even if you are trying to cook and eat lighter, it does not mean you need to give up hearty comfort food. This chili is made healthier by using turkey—in two different forms—and loads of beans and veggies. The ground turkey makes the chili hearty and filling. The smoked turkey sausage adds a meaty texture and savory flavor. This chili is the epitome of comfort food but also works as a healthy weeknight meal.

YIELD: 8 SERVINGS

2 tbsp (30 ml) extra virgin olive oil, divided

1 small white onion, diced

¾ cup (112 g) diced mini sweet peppers (any color or combination of colors)

4 cloves garlic, coarsely chopped

1 lb (454 g) 93 percent lean ground turkey

2 tbsp (18 g) chili powder

2 tsp (6 g) ground cumin

2 tsp (6 g) smoked paprika

1 tsp dried oregano

1½ tsp (8 g) salt

½ tsp black pepper

¼ tsp cayenne pepper

¼ cup (66 g) tomato paste

1 (28-oz [794-g]) can crushed San Marzano tomatoes

1 cup (240 ml) chicken broth

½ tbsp (5 g) brown sugar

2 tbsp (30 ml) Worcestershire sauce

1 (15-oz [425-g]) can corn, drained and rinsed

1 (15-oz [425-g]) can black beans, drained and rinsed

1 (15-oz [425-g]) can kidney beans, drained and rinsed

1 (13-oz [369-g]) smoked kielbasa turkey sausage (such as Hillshire Farm® brand), thinly sliced

½ cup (143 g) plain Greek yogurt

½ cup (60 g) shredded Cheddar cheese

½ cup (32 g) crushed tortilla chips (such as Beanitos brand)

2 tbsp (6 g) finely chopped fresh cilantro

Hot sauce, as needed (optional)

Heat 1 tablespoon (15 ml) of the oil in a large pot or Dutch oven over medium-high heat. Add the onion and sweet peppers and sauté them for 5 to 7 minutes, stirring frequently. Lower the heat to medium and add the garlic. Cook the vegetables for 2 to 3 minutes, or until the garlic is fragrant.

Add the ground turkey and cook it for 3 to 5 minutes, or until it is no longer pink, breaking it up as it cooks. Add the chili powder, cumin, smoked paprika, oregano, salt, black pepper and cayenne pepper, and cook the mixture for about 20 seconds, until the spices are fragrant and coat the meat.

Add the tomato paste and cook the mixture for 1 to 2 minutes, until the tomato paste turns a rusty red color.

Add the crushed tomatoes, broth, brown sugar, Worcestershire sauce, corn, black beans and kidney beans. Bring the chili to a boil, then reduce the heat to medium-low and simmer the chili for 45 to 60 minutes, or until the chili thickens and the flavors come together. Adjust the seasonings as necessary.

Heat the remaining 1 tablespoon (15 ml) of the oil in a large skillet over medium-high heat. Add the turkey sausage and cook it for 2 to 3 minutes, until a golden-brown crust forms on each side. Add the sausage to the chili.

Garnish the chili with the yogurt, Cheddar cheese, tortilla chips, cilantro and hot sauce (if using).

FETA AND MOZZARELLA-STUFFED CHICKEN BURGERS WITH SUN-DRIED TOMATO AIOLI

I tested this recipe for my parents and got a big thumbs-up. This was a huge feat, because my mom typically does not like chicken burgers. Ground chicken is a great alternative to beef, as it has less fat and cholesterol. But ground chicken can be boring and dry. It needs a little love to make it shine. I did several things to liven up the ground chicken for this recipe. For starters, I used a combination of ground chicken and chicken sausage—the addition of a little sausage adds flavor and moisture to the lean ground chicken. Next, I used two different kinds of breadcrumbs to add texture and flavor. Third, I stuffed these burgers with feta and fresh mozzarella, so that when you bite into them you find a gooey, delicious surprise. Finally, I topped these burgers with a creamy, bright and bold sun-dried tomato aioli. These burgers are anything but boring!

YIELD: 4 BURGERS

Burgers

1 lb (454 g) 93 percent lean ground chicken

8 oz (227 g) ground Italian chicken sausage

⅓ cup (30 g) whole-wheat panko breadcrumbs

½ cup (61 g) Italian breadcrumbs

1 large egg

3 to 4 cloves garlic, finely chopped

1 tsp salt

½ tsp black pepper

4 (½" [13-mm])-thick round slices fresh mozzarella cheese

½ cup (75 g) crumbled feta cheese, divided

2 tbsp (30 ml) extra virgin olive oil, divided

4 whole-wheat or brioche buns

1 cup (20 g) arugula

To make the burgers, combine the ground chicken, chicken sausage, panko breadcrumbs, Italian breadcrumbs, egg, garlic, salt and black pepper in a large bowl. Gently mix the ingredients together. Allow the burger mixture to rest for 10 to 15 minutes.

Divide the burger mixture into four portions. The mixture will be slightly sticky, but this is normal. Take each portion and make two thin patties that are larger in circumference than the slices of mozzarella cheese. Place a slice of mozzarella on top of a patty. Add 1 tablespoon (10 g) of the feta cheese on top of the mozzarella. Place the other patty on top and seal the sides so the patties become one burger and enclose the cheeses. Repeat this process until you have four stuffed burgers.

Place the burgers in the refrigerator to chill for at least 30 minutes.

(Continued)

Sun-Dried Tomato Aioli

⅓ cup (73 g) olive oil mayo

2 tbsp (36 g) plain Greek yogurt

¼ cup (28 g) julienned sun-dried tomatoes packed in olive oil, drained

1 tbsp (15 ml) fresh lemon juice

¼ tsp salt

Pinch of black pepper

Meanwhile, make the sun-dried tomato aioli by combining the mayo, yogurt, sun-dried tomatoes, lemon juice, salt and black pepper in a food processor. Process the ingredients until the sun-dried tomatoes are broken down into small pieces. Set the aioli aside.

Preheat the oven to 400°F (204°C). Grease a medium baking sheet.

Heat 1½ tablespoons (23 ml) of the oil in a large cast-iron skillet over medium-high heat. Add the burgers and cook them for 3 to 4 minutes on each side, or until a golden-brown crust forms on each side. Transfer the burgers to the prepared baking sheet.

Bake the burgers in the oven for 6 to 8 minutes, or until their internal temperature reaches 165°F (74°C). Allow the burgers to rest for 5 minutes after removing them from the oven.

Meanwhile, wipe out the skillet so the chicken juices are removed. Add the remaining ½ tablespoon (7 ml) of oil and return the skillet to medium heat.

Toast the buns in the skillet for 1 to 2 minutes per side, until both sides are golden brown. Slather each of the buns with the sun-dried tomato aioli. Top the bottom bun with the arugula, a burger patty and the remaining feta, if desired, then top the burger with the other half of the bun.

CHICKEN SHAWARMA AND QUINOA BOWLS

This is a fun, healthier spin on a classic Middle Eastern dish. Chicken shawarma is a popular Middle Eastern street food that typically consists of thin cuts of seasoned chicken cooked slowly on a skewer and served in a warm pita. I take all of those delicious flavors to make this nutrient-dense and flavorful bowl. Chicken is a popular dinner protein option when it comes to lean protein, as it packs a considerable amount into a single serving without a lot of fat. I use chicken breast marinated in an assertive marinade full of traditional spices like turmeric, cardamom, cinnamon, cumin and smoked paprika. Then the chicken is grilled to perfection, keeping it tender and juicy. The chicken is paired with quinoa, a nutrient-rich ancient grain and tons of veggies. Finally, it's topped with a bright, creamy balsamic-tahini dressing. This bowl is bursting with big, bold flavors and tastes amazing!

YIELD: 4 SERVINGS

Chicken

1½ lb (680 g) boneless, skinless chicken breasts

½ cup (120 ml) extra virgin olive oil

4 cloves garlic, coarsely chopped

1½ tsp (8 g) salt

2 tsp (6 g) ground cumin

2 tsp (6 g) smoked paprika

1 tsp ground coriander

½ tsp ground cardamom

½ tsp ground turmeric

½ tsp ground cinnamon

½ tsp black pepper

Balsamic-Tahini Dressing

½ cup (112 g) tahini

2 tbsp (30 ml) extra virgin olive oil

2 tbsp (30 ml) good-quality balsamic vinegar

2 tsp (10 ml) agave or pure maple syrup

1 tsp Dijon mustard

½ tsp salt

½ tsp black pepper

2 to 4 tbsp (30 to 60 ml) water

To make the chicken, use a meat tenderizer to pound the chicken breasts until they are about 1 inch (3 cm) thick. Place the chicken in a ziplock bag.

In a small bowl, whisk together the oil, garlic, salt, cumin, smoked paprika, coriander, cardamom, turmeric, cinnamon and black pepper. Pour the marinade over the chicken. Seal the ziplock bag and place the chicken in the refrigerator to marinate for at least 1 hour but preferably overnight.

Remove the chicken from the refrigerator about 1 hour before you will be grilling it.

Preheat the grill to about 400°F (204°C). Cook the chicken for 4 to 5 minutes on each side, or until it achieves grill marks and its internal temperature reaches 165°F (74°C). Remove the chicken from the grill and allow it to rest for 5 to 10 minutes. Cut the chicken into strips of your preferred thickness.

To make the balsamic-tahini dressing, whisk together the tahini, oil, vinegar, agave, mustard, salt and black pepper in a small bowl until the mixture is smooth. Add the water, 1 tablespoon (15 ml) at a time, until you reach your desired consistency. Set the dressing aside.

(Continued)

Bowls

1½ cups (255 g) quinoa, cooked

½ tsp salt

¼ tsp black pepper

½ tbsp (8 ml) extra virgin olive oil

2 cups (40 g) arugula

¾ cup (131 g) halved cherry tomatoes

½ cup (65 g) pickled red onions (page 93)

1 medium avocado, thinly sliced

½ cup (75 g) crumbled feta cheese

To make the bowls, season the quinoa with the salt, black pepper and oil. Stir the quinoa.

Divide the quinoa, arugula, tomatoes, pickled red onions, avocado, chicken strips and feta cheese among four bowls. Top each serving with the desired amount of the balsamic-tahini dressing.

SOUTHWEST TURKEY SAUSAGE BREAKFAST BURRITOS

Burritos are not just for lunch or dinner—they are perfect for breakfast too. These breakfast burritos are made healthier with turkey sausage and are packed with bold southwestern flavors. Turkey sausage is a great alternative to fatty pork sausage. It's still juicy and flavorful but contains a lot less fat and fewer calories. These burritos are also filled with perfectly scrambled, super cheesy eggs and creamy, ripe avocados. This meal is the perfect nutrient-packed and flavorful breakfast—or breakfast for dinner!

YIELD: 6 BURRITOS

2 tbsp (30 ml) avocado oil or neutral oil of choice, divided

6 links precooked turkey sausage, thawed (such as Applegate brand)

½ cup (76 g) diced red onion

½ cup (75 g) diced mini sweet peppers (any color or combination of colors)

2 to 3 cloves garlic, coarsely chopped

½ tsp chili powder

¼ tsp ground cumin

¾ tsp salt, divided

8 large eggs

1 tbsp (15 ml) milk or water

½ cup (56 g) shredded pepper Jack cheese

¼ tsp black pepper

6 (8" [20-cm]) whole-wheat tortillas

1 medium avocado, diced

1 to 2 tbsp (15 to 30 ml) hot sauce (optional)

Heat 1 tablespoon (15 ml) of the oil in a large skillet over medium heat. Add the sausage links and cook them for 3 to 5 minutes, until they are golden brown on the outside and warmed all the way through. Remove the sausage from the skillet and cut the links into small pieces.

Return the skillet to medium heat and add ½ tablespoon (8 ml) of the oil. Add the onion and sweet peppers and cook the vegetables for 3 to 5 minutes, until they are caramelized. Add the garlic, chili powder, cumin and ½ teaspoon of the salt and cook the mixture for 2 to 3 minutes, until the spices are fragrant. Remove the vegetable mixture from the skillet and wipe the skillet clean.

In a medium bowl, whisk together the eggs and milk. Heat the remaining ½ tablespoon (8 ml) of oil in the skillet over medium-low heat. Add the eggs and cook them for 5 to 7 minutes, until curds form and the eggs are softly scrambled. During the final minute of cooking, add the pepper Jack cheese and the remaining ¼ teaspoon of salt and black pepper.

Once the eggs are cooked, gently fold in the vegetable mixture.

Microwave the tortillas for 20 to 30 seconds, until they are warm and pliable.

Divide the egg mixture, sausage, avocado and hot sauce (if using) among the tortillas. Wrap each tortilla into a burrito.

Note: These burritos freeze well. Just allow them to cool completely, wrap them tightly in foil, label the foil with a permanent marker and add all the foil-wrapped burritos to an airtight freezer bag. They will last about 1 month in the freezer. When you are ready to eat, remove the foil from a burrito and microwave it for 3 to 5 minutes, or until it is warmed all the way through.

SPICY BUTTERMILK RANCH "FRIED" CHICKEN

Who doesn't love fried chicken? That crunchy exterior and juicy interior—fried chicken is addictively delicious. Traditional fried chicken is not very healthy, because it's fried in oil and heavily breaded. So I created a baked "fried" chicken coated in whole-wheat flour and whole-wheat panko breadcrumbs. I tested this recipe several times to get it just right, and I'm sharing those secrets with you!

YIELD: 4 TO 6 SERVINGS

Spicy Buttermilk Chicken

1 cup (240 ml) buttermilk

½ tsp paprika

½ tsp garlic powder

½ tsp onion powder

⅛ tsp ground nutmeg

½ tsp salt

¼ tsp black pepper

1 to 2 tsp (5 to 10 ml) hot sauce

2 lb (908 g) boneless, skinless chicken breasts

1½ tbsp (23 ml) extra virgin olive oil

Ranch Coating

1 large egg

¾ cup (98 g) whole-wheat flour

½ cup (45 g) whole-wheat panko breadcrumbs

½ tsp baking powder

1 tsp garlic powder

1 tsp dried onion flakes

½ tsp dried dill

½ tsp paprika

1½ tsp (8 g) salt

½ tsp black pepper

½ tsp Italian seasoning

To make the spicy buttermilk chicken, combine the buttermilk, paprika, garlic powder, onion powder, nutmeg, salt, black pepper and hot sauce in a large ziplock bag or lidded bowl. Mix until all of the ingredients are well incorporated to form a marinade. Add the chicken breasts and seal the bag or container. Transfer the chicken to the refrigerator and allow it to marinate for at least 4 hours but preferably overnight.

Set out a large baking sheet and spray it with cooking spray. Remove the chicken from the marinade and shake off the excess buttermilk. Transfer the chicken to the baking sheet. Do not discard the marinade.

Preheat the oven to 425°F (218°C). Put another large baking sheet in the oven while it preheats.

To make the ranch coating, whisk together the egg and ⅓ cup (80 ml) of the marinade in a wide, shallow bowl.

In another wide, shallow bowl, whisk together the flour, breadcrumbs, baking powder, garlic powder, onion flakes, dill, paprika, salt, black pepper and Italian seasoning until the ingredients are well combined.

To coat the chicken breasts, first dip the chicken into the breadcrumb mixture and make sure it's completely covered in the coating. Next, dip the chicken into the egg mixture so it's completely coated. Finally, dip the chicken again in the coating mixture so it's completely breaded. Shake off any excess coating. Place the coated chicken on the cold baking sheet. Repeat this process until all of the chicken is fully coated.

Allow the chicken to rest on the baking sheet for at least 30 minutes. This allows the coating to completely adhere to the chicken.

Remove the other baking sheet from the oven. Drizzle the baking sheet with the oil. Transfer the chicken to the baking sheet.

Bake the chicken for 18 to 22 minutes, flipping it halfway through the baking time, until it is golden brown and crispy. Allow the chicken to rest for 5 minutes.

Note: This "fried" chicken pairs wonderfully with my Roasted Garlic and Cream Cheese Mashed Cauliflower (page 109)!

JAMAICAN JERK GRILLED CHICKEN WRAPS

A homemade jerk seasoning and a citrus-forward marinade bring tons of flavor to perfectly grilled chicken thighs. To create a delectable Caribbean-inspired lunch, the chicken is paired with a fresh, crunchy slaw and jerk-seasoned aioli and wrapped in a whole-wheat tortilla. This simple yet flavorful dish will transport you right to the islands!

YIELD: 6 TO 8 WRAPS

Spice Blend

1 tbsp (9 g) garlic powder

1 tbsp (9 g) onion powder

1½ tsp (5 g) cayenne pepper

2 tsp (6 g) smoked paprika

1 tsp ground cinnamon

1 tsp ground allspice

½ tsp ground nutmeg

2 tsp (2 g) dried parsley

2 tsp (2 g) dried thyme

1 tbsp (12 g) coconut sugar or brown sugar

2 tsp (10 g) salt

½ tsp black pepper

1 tsp ground cumin

Marinade

½ cup (120 ml) extra virgin olive oil

2 tbsp (30 ml) soy sauce

1 tsp Worcestershire sauce

1 tbsp (9 g) minced garlic

Zest and juice of 1 medium lime

Zest and juice of 1 medium orange

3½ tbsp (32 g) spice blend

1½ lb (680 g) boneless, skinless chicken thighs

¼ tsp salt

To make the spice blend, combine the garlic powder, onion powder, cayenne pepper, smoked paprika, cinnamon, allspice, nutmeg, parsley, thyme, sugar, salt, black pepper and cumin in a small bowl. Stir until the spices are well combined. This recipe makes more than you will need for the wraps; store the extra spice blend in an airtight container for up to 1 year.

To make the marinade, combine the oil, soy sauce, Worcestershire sauce, garlic, lime zest, lime juice, orange zest, orange juice and the spice blend in a small bowl. Stir until the ingredients are well combined.

Place the chicken thighs in a large ziplock bag or lidded container. Pour the marinade over the chicken thighs, making sure all of the chicken is coated. Seal the bag or container and place it in the refrigerator for at least 1 hour but preferably 6 to 8 hours. Remove the chicken from the refrigerator at least 30 minutes before grilling it.

(Continued)

Slaw

Juice of 1 medium lime

2 tbsp (30 ml) apple cider vinegar

1 tbsp (15 ml) agave

1 tsp Worcestershire sauce

½ tsp salt

Pinch of black pepper

3½ cups (700 g) shredded coleslaw mix

2 tbsp (6 g) coarsely chopped fresh cilantro

Lime-Jerk Aioli

½ cup (143 g) plain Greek yogurt

¼ cup (110 g) olive oil mayo

1 to 2 tsp (3 to 6 g) spice blend

Pinch of salt

1 tbsp (15 ml) fresh lime juice

Dash of Worcestershire sauce

Wraps

6 to 8 (8" [20-cm]) whole-wheat tortillas

To make the slaw, whisk together the lime juice, vinegar, agave, Worcestershire sauce, salt and black pepper in a large bowl. Add the coleslaw mix and cilantro and stir until they are thoroughly coated in the dressing. Set the slaw aside.

To make the lime-jerk aioli, whisk together the yogurt, mayo, the spice blend, salt, lime juice and Worcestershire sauce in a small bowl.

Preheat the grill to 375°F (191°C). Alternatively, preheat a large grill pan over medium-high heat. Grill the chicken for 4 to 5 minutes per side, until it achieves grill marks and a charred crust on the outside and its internal temperature reaches 165°F (74°C). Remove the chicken from the grill and sprinkle it with the salt and a dash of the spice blend. Allow the chicken to rest for 5 minutes. Cut the chicken into thin strips.

To build the wraps, spread some of the aioli on a tortilla. Top the aioli with the chicken strips and slaw. Roll the tortilla up tightly. Cut the wrap in half to serve.

Note: Boneless and skinless chicken thighs are slightly more tender and flavorful than chicken breast due to their higher fat content, but they are still a lean, low-calorie meat.

Extra Swaps: I use whole-wheat wraps instead of white-flour tortillas in this recipe, as they add healthy whole grains and extra fiber to the meal. I also subbed Greek yogurt for some of the mayo in the sauce to reduce the fat content and up the protein.

HEALTHY CHICKEN PARMESAN

Chicken Parmesan is a hearty, delicious, nostalgic family dinner I adore. However, it typically involves chicken fried in canola oil and served with starchy pasta. I knew this Italian classic could use a healthy makeover. To lighten it up, I bread the chicken in whole-wheat breadcrumbs instead of white breadcrumbs to add fiber and then I lightly fry it in nutrient-rich olive oil instead of canola oil. These two simple swaps create a chicken breast that is still crunchy, moist and flavor-packed but much less caloric!

YIELD: 4 TO 6 SERVINGS

Red Sauce and Pasta

2 tbsp (30 ml) extra virgin olive oil, divided

1 small white onion, diced

1 tbsp (9 g) finely chopped garlic

2 tsp (6 g) garlic powder

2 tsp (2 g) dried basil

1½ tsp (2 g) dried oregano

1 tsp dried parsley

1 tsp onion powder

2 tsp (10 g) salt

¼ cup (60 g) tomato paste

1 (28-oz [794-g]) can crushed tomatoes

1 (28-oz [828-ml]) can tomato sauce

1 tbsp (15 ml) balsamic vinegar

1 lb (454 g) whole-wheat or gluten-free spaghetti (I like Banza), cooked according to package instructions

To make the red sauce and pasta, heat 1 tablespoon (15 ml) of the oil in a large Dutch oven or pot over medium heat. Add the onion and cook it for 3 to 5 minutes, or until the onion softens and becomes translucent. Add the garlic and the remaining 1 tablespoon (15 ml) of oil if the Dutch oven is dry. Cook the mixture for 1 to 2 minutes, or until the garlic is fragrant. Add the garlic powder, basil, oregano, parsley, onion powder, salt and tomato paste. Cook the mixture for 1 to 2 minutes.

Add the crushed tomatoes, tomato sauce and vinegar and bring the sauce to a low boil. Reduce the heat to medium-low and simmer the sauce for 20 to 30 minutes, so that it slowly develops its flavor.

(Continued)

Chicken Parmesan

2 large eggs

½ tbsp (8 ml) water

3 tbsp (45 ml) extra virgin olive oil, divided

1 cup (121 g) whole-wheat breadcrumbs

½ cup (90 g) grated Parmesan cheese

2 tsp (10 g) salt

½ tsp black pepper

1 tsp garlic powder

½ tsp onion powder

1½ tsp (2 g) Italian seasoning

4 to 6 boneless, skinless chicken breasts, patted dry

4 to 6 large leaves fresh basil

4 to 6 (1" [3-cm])-thick slices fresh mozzarella cheese

To make the chicken Parmesan, set out two wide, shallow bowls. Set out a large baking sheet next to the bowls.

In the first bowl, combine the eggs, water and 1 tablespoon (15 ml) of the oil. Whisk the ingredients until the eggs are fully combined with the water and oil. In the second bowl, stir together the breadcrumbs, Parmesan cheese, salt, black pepper, garlic powder, onion powder and Italian seasoning.

Dip each chicken breast into the egg mixture and then the breadcrumb mixture, so that the chicken is entirely coated. Place the chicken on the baking sheet. Allow the chicken to rest for at least 10 minutes, so the breadcrumbs can fully adhere to the meat.

Heat the remaining 2 tablespoons (30 ml) of oil in a large lidded skillet over medium heat. Add the chicken breasts and cook them for 3 to 4 minutes per side, until each side is golden brown. Top each chicken breast with a little of the red sauce, 1 basil leaf and 1 slice of the mozzarella cheese. Cover the skillet with its lid and cook the chicken for 1 to 2 minutes, or until the cheese is fully melted. Remove the chicken from the skillet.

Place the desired amount of spaghetti on each plate, then top the spaghetti with the red sauce and a chicken breast.

Note: This recipe won't use all the red sauce. Store leftover sauce in an air-tight container in the fridge for 1 to 2 weeks.

Extra Swaps: The red sauce is made from scratch with only wholesome, real ingredients—no preservatives or hidden sugars typically found in the store-bought kinds. I also use a gluten-free, chickpea-based pasta that's full of protein and fiber instead of white, starchy spaghetti.

CHICKEN SAUSAGE AND VEGGIE SHEET PAN MEAL

This is one of my go-to weeknight meals—it's simple, quick, delicious and made with healthy, wholesome ingredients. I use chicken sausage in place of fatty pork sausage to keep this meal lean and light. There are so many great, high-quality brands of chicken sausage available today in a variety of different flavors. Pick your favorite sausage, along with your favorite veggies, a drizzle of olive oil and a few spices for a crowd-pleasing, healthy, easy dinner.

YIELD: 4 SERVINGS

Chicken Sausage and Vegetables

4 links precooked chicken sausage links, sliced into 1" (3-cm)-thick rounds

1 medium head broccoli, cut into medium-sized florets

1 medium yellow bell pepper, cut into medium-sized chunks

1 small red onion, cut into medium-sized chunks

2 tbsp (30 ml) extra virgin olive oil

1 tsp garlic powder

1 tsp onion powder

1 tsp salt

1 tsp Italian seasoning

Black pepper, as needed

Lemon-Tahini Sauce

½ cup (224 g) tahini

Juice of ½ medium lemon

1 tsp Dijon mustard

1½ tbsp (23 ml) pure maple syrup

Dash of Worcestershire sauce

½ tsp garlic powder

½ tsp salt

2 to 6 tbsp (30 to 90 ml) water

To make the chicken sausage and vegetables, preheat the oven to 400°F (204°C). Lightly grease a large baking sheet.

In a large ziplock bag or bowl, combine the sausage, broccoli, bell pepper, onion, oil, garlic powder, onion powder, salt, Italian seasoning and black pepper. Shake the bag or stir the mixture to coat the sausage and vegetables in the oil and seasonings. Transfer the mixture to the prepared baking sheet. Roast the sausage and vegetables for 25 to 30 minutes, flipping everything halfway through the roasting time, until the vegetables are slightly charred and the sausage forms a golden-brown crust.

To make the lemon-tahini sauce, combine the tahini, lemon juice, mustard, maple syrup, Worcestershire, garlic powder and salt in a small bowl. Stir the ingredients well; the mixture will be thick. Thin the sauce with the water, 1 tablespoon (15 ml) at a time, until you've reached your desired consistency.

Divide the sausage and vegetables among four plates and drizzle each serving with the lemon-tahini sauce.

Note: This meal is great served with brown rice or quinoa.

Extra Swap: The lemon-tahini sauce is sweetened with only maple syrup, so it is refined sugar–free.

ALTERNATIVE FLOURS—HAVE YOUR CAKE AND EAT IT TOO!

The Swap: Alternative, nutrient-rich flours instead of white, starchy flour.

Swapping white refined flour for nutritious alternative flours allows you to have your healthier cake and eat it too!

There are several reasons why we should try to minimize white flour in our diets. For starters, it's void of any nutritional value. This means that white flour has been stripped of its vitamins, minerals and dietary fiber. Most white flour also goes through a bleaching process in which benzoyl peroxide, potassium bromate or chlorine is added to make it whiter in appearance, so we are consuming unnecessary chemicals. On top of all that, refined white flour is known to spike blood sugar levels.

Before you panic and start saying goodbye to your favorite breads, pastas and desserts, I want to introduce you to some wonderful alternative flours that allow you to enjoy the foods you love while still being good to your body!

Some of my favorite healthy substitutes that you will find in this chapter are oat flour, whole-wheat flour, coconut flour, almond flour and chickpea flour. All of these flours taste great and can produce delicious recipes while simultaneously supplementing our nutritional intake.

Oat flour is simply ground rolled oats and can be gluten-free if you use gluten-free oats. Oat flour is high in fiber and protein. It has a very similar texture to white flour, can be made easily and cheaply at home and has a subtle nutty flavor that enhances the recipe without overpowering it.

Whole-wheat flour is made by grinding the entire grain, including the bran and germ, so it's packed with protein, fiber, vitamins and minerals. Whole-wheat flour can usually be swapped seamlessly with white flour, making it an easy-to-use alternative. It also provides a nutty, hearty flavor to baked goods and savory treats.

Almond flour is made by peeling almonds and grinding them into a fine powder. It's high in fiber, healthy fats and vitamins, like vitamin E and magnesium. Almond flour is naturally gluten-free. It has a delicious nutty flavor that works beautifully in desserts and other baked goods. It also works well as breadcrumbs, because its coarser consistency helps achieve a light, crispy crust.

Coconut flour is made from ground, dried coconut flesh. It's packed with healthy fats, fiber and protein and is gluten-free. It adds a delicate coconut flavor to foods and, because of its sweeter taste, allows you to use less sugar to achieve the right amount of sweetness in baked goods. Note that coconut flour is more absorbent than other alternative flours, so it requires more liquid to achieve the correct consistency in the final product.

Finally, chickpea flour is made from dried roasted chickpeas (i.e., garbanzo beans). Chickpeas are a great source of vitamins, minerals and fiber. Chickpea flour has a relatively neutral flavor, allowing for a seamless swap. It generally can be used as a one-to-one substitute for white flour. It works well in baked goods and works great in savory dishes as a binder or thickener for sauces.

I understand that using new flours can be intimidating. Some flours are an easy one-to-one swap with regular white flour, while others, due to their different textures and densities, may not swap as easily. No need to fear or avoid alternative flours—I will show you how to use each of my favorite flours to make foods like muffins, chicken tenders, meatloaf and of course, cake!

MINI TURKEY MEATLOAVES

These incredibly moist and flavorful mini turkey meatloaves have a secret ingredient: ground oats. The oats replace the breadcrumbs, making this recipe a gluten-free meal. The oats help bind the meatloaves but are undetectable—a great way to add nutrients and whole grains to a dish. These mini meatloaves are seasoned with flavorful spices and kept tender with the help of grated onion. They are baked in a muffin pan for individual servings and topped with a tangy-yet-sweet sauce. This dish proves that meatloaf is anything but boring and will have your family demanding seconds!

YIELD: 9 SERVINGS

Mini Meatloaves

1 large egg

1 tbsp (18 g) low-sugar, minimally processed ketchup (such as Sir Kensington's brand)

1 tbsp (15 ml) Worcestershire sauce

1 tbsp (15 ml) Dani's Famous Barbecue Sauce (page 135) or low-sugar store-bought barbecue sauce

½ small white onion, grated

1 lb (454 g) 93 percent lean ground turkey

¾ cup (68 g) oat flour (see Notes)

1 tsp garlic powder

¾ tsp onion powder

1 tsp Italian seasoning

¼ tsp cayenne pepper

½ tsp mustard powder

1 tsp salt

½ tsp black pepper

Sauce

½ cup (144 g) low-sugar, minimally processed ketchup (such as Sir Kensington's brand)

1½ tbsp (14 g) brown sugar

½ tbsp (8 ml) apple cider vinegar

1 tsp Dijon mustard

2 tsp (10 ml) Worcestershire sauce

To make the mini meatloaves, preheat the oven to 375°F (191°C). Grease nine cavities in a twelve-cavity muffin pan.

In a large bowl, whisk together the egg, ketchup, Worcestershire sauce, Dani's Famous Barbecue Sauce and onion. Add the ground turkey and mix the ingredients together until the turkey is mostly incorporated.

In a small bowl, combine the flour, garlic powder, onion powder, Italian seasoning, cayenne pepper, mustard powder, salt and black pepper. Add the flour mixture to the turkey mixture and mix until the ingredients are well combined. Allow the meatloaf mixture to rest for 10 minutes.

To make the sauce, whisk together the ketchup, brown sugar, vinegar, mustard and Worcestershire sauce in a small bowl. Set the sauce aside.

Divide the meatloaf mixture among the prepared muffin cavities. Bake the meatloaves for 16 minutes. Pat the tops of the meatloaves dry, as they will have released juices as they have cooked. Top each meatloaf with some of the sauce. Bake the meatloaves for 6 to 8 minutes, or until the meatloaves' internal temperature reaches 165°F (74°C).

Allow the meatloaves to rest for 5 minutes before removing them from the muffin pan.

Notes: To make oat flour, simply grind rolled oats in a food processor until they resemble breadcrumbs.

These mini meatloaves pair well with the Roasted Garlic and Cream Cheese Mashed Cauliflower (page 109).

ALMOND FLOUR CHICKEN TENDERS

Alternative flours are not just for baking. You can use them in savory cooking as well! Almond flour is perfect for crusting chicken to make it super crispy and flavorful. I use almonds two ways in this recipe. First, I use blanched almond flour to initially coat the chicken. Second, I add crushed almonds for extra crunchy "breading." The chicken is then baked to golden-brown perfection and served with a homemade Greek yogurt ranch for dipping. Best of all, this dish is kid-friendly!

YIELD: 4 TO 6 SERVINGS

Almond Flour Chicken Tenders

1½ cups (138 g) unsalted sliced almonds

¾ cup (72 g) blanched almond flour

1 tsp salt

2 large eggs

2 tsp (10 g) Dijon mustard

1 tsp Worcestershire sauce

1½ tsp (5 g) garlic salt

2 tsp (2 g) Italian seasoning

¼ tsp paprika

¼ to ½ tsp Hungarian hot paprika or cayenne pepper

1½ lb (680 g) chicken tenderloins

½ tbsp (8 ml) extra virgin olive oil

Spicy Greek Yogurt Ranch

½ cup (143 g) plain Greek yogurt

2 tbsp (28 g) olive oil mayo

1 to 2 tsp (5 to 10 ml) hot sauce

1 tsp Worcestershire sauce

½ tbsp (8 ml) lemon juice

½ tsp garlic salt

½ tsp onion powder

½ tsp dried parsley

¼ tsp Hungarian hot paprika or cayenne pepper

1 to 2 tbsp (15 to 30 ml) unsweetened plain almond milk, cashew milk or buttermilk

To make the almond flour chicken tenders, preheat the oven to 425°F (218°C). Place a large oven-safe cooling rack over a large baking sheet. Grease the rack well.

Place the sliced almonds in a food processor and process them until they reach a crumbly, sand-like consistency.

Create a breading station by arranging three wide, shallow bowls in a row. In the first bowl, combine the almond flour and salt. In the second bowl, combine the eggs, mustard and Worcestershire sauce and whisk until the ingredients are well combined. In the third bowl, combine the crushed almonds, garlic salt, Italian seasoning, paprika and Hungarian hot paprika.

Coat a chicken tenderloin with the almond flour mixture, then dip it in the egg wash and then coat it with the crushed almond mixture. Place the chicken on the prepared rack. Repeat this process until all of the chicken tenderloins are "breaded." Allow the chicken to rest for 10 minutes so the breading can properly adhere.

Brush a little of the oil on each chicken tenderloin. Bake the chicken for 8 minutes, then flip the tenderloins, brush on more oil and bake the chicken for 8 to 10 minutes, or until the chicken's internal temperature reaches 165°F (74°C) and the meat is no longer pink in the middle.

For an extra crispy option, increase the oven's temperature to broil and cook the chicken for 1 to 2 minutes per side, or until the nuts are golden brown.

To make the spicy Greek yogurt ranch, whisk together the yogurt, mayo, hot sauce, Worcestershire sauce, lemon juice, garlic salt, onion powder, parsley and Hungarian hot paprika in a medium bowl. Add the almond milk, 1 tablespoon (15 ml) at a time, until you reach your desired consistency.

Serve the chicken tenders with the ranch.

Extra Swap: The spicy Greek yogurt ranch replaces most of the mayo in traditional ranch dressing with protein-rich Greek yogurt.

WHOLE-WHEAT AND OAT GARLIC KNOTS

For this dish, soft and airy pizza dough knots are covered in garlic butter and baked until they are golden. I replace white flour with white whole-wheat flour and oat flour, which add protein and fiber but still create tender knots. The knots are packed with garlic flavor, both in the dough and the melted butter on top. I taste tested these on my one-year-old son, Grayson, and after one bite he exclaimed, Mmmmm! A good sign that these are quite delicious!

YIELD: 14 TO 16 KNOTS

Garlic Knots

1¼ cups (300 ml) warm water (100 to 110°F [38 to 43°C])

2¼ tsp (7 g) active dry yeast

1 tbsp (12 g) organic granulated sugar

2½ tbsp (38 ml) extra virgin olive oil, divided

1 tsp salt

2 cups (260 g) white whole-wheat flour, plus more as needed

1 cup (90 g) oat flour

2 tsp (6 g) garlic powder

¼ cup (45 g) grated Parmesan cheese

2 to 3 tbsp (6 to 9 g) coarsely chopped fresh basil

½ cup (120 ml) red sauce (page 35) or store-bought marinara sauce (optional)

Garlic Butter

5 tbsp (75 ml) melted unsalted butter

1 tsp Italian seasoning

2 tbsp (18 g) finely chopped garlic

½ tsp garlic salt

Note: You can also divide the dough in half and make two 10-inch (25-cm) pizzas. Just top the dough with your favorite toppings and bake them at 450°F (232°C) for 18 to 22 minutes.

To make the garlic knots, whisk the water, yeast and sugar together in the bowl of a stand mixer fitted with a dough hook or paddle attachment. Cover the bowl and allow the mixture to rest for 5 minutes. The yeast will activate and bubble at the top.

Add 2 tablespoons (30 ml) of the oil, salt and white whole-wheat flour. Beat the mixture on medium-low speed for 15 seconds, then add the oat flour and garlic powder. Beat the mixture on low speed for 2 minutes.

Lightly dust a work surface with additional white whole-wheat flour. Transfer the dough to the prepared work surface. Knead the dough for 3 to 4 minutes. After kneading, the dough should still feel a little soft. Poke it with your finger—if the dough slowly bounces back, it is ready to rise.

Coat a large bowl or the bowl of the stand mixer with oil and drizzle the remaining ½ tablespoon (8 ml) of oil over the dough ball. Place the dough ball in the prepared bowl and cover it with a towel. Place the bowl in a warm place and allow the dough to rest for 1 to 2 hours; it will double in size.

Grease a large baking sheet. Lightly dust a work surface with additional white whole-wheat flour. When the dough is ready, punch it down to release the air. Transfer the dough to the prepared work surface. Shape the dough into a long log shape that is 15 to 16 inches (38 to 40 cm) long and 4 to 5 inches (10 to 12.5 cm) wide. Using a sharp knife, pizza cutter or pastry scraper, slice the log into 14 to 16 (1- to 2-inch [2.5- to 5-cm])-wide strips. Roll each strip into a rope that is 6 to 8 inches (15 to 20 cm) long. Tie each into a knot and attach the ends to the sides (see photo).

Place the knots on the prepared baking sheet. Lightly cover the knots with a clean towel and let them rest for 30 to 45 minutes. They will puff up slightly during this time. While the knots rest, preheat the oven to 400°F (204°C).

To make the garlic butter, combine the butter, Italian seasoning, garlic and garlic salt in a small bowl. Pour some of the garlic butter over each knot, reserving a little for topping the knots later. Bake the garlic knots for 18 to 22 minutes, or until they are golden brown on top.

Remove the garlic knots from the oven and brush the warm knots with the remaining garlic butter. Sprinkle them with the Parmesan cheese and basil. Serve the garlic knots with the red sauce (if using).

THE BEST HEALTHIER BANANA BREAD

This incredibly moist banana bread is made with whole-wheat pastry flour and oat flour. These are the two main flours you will find in my pantry; mixed together, they create a tender, delicate crumb just like white flour. In addition, whole-wheat and oat flours add fiber and protein to recipes, making your favorite baked goods a little more nutritious. These muffins are a delicious and healthy breakfast treat perfect for busy mornings. They are a favorite of my son Grayson!

YIELD: 1 (9 X 5-INCH [23 X 13-CM]) BANANA BREAD LOAF

1 cup (120 g) whole-wheat pastry flour (see Notes)

½ cup (45 g) oat flour

1 tsp baking soda

½ tsp salt

¼ tsp ground nutmeg

1 tsp ground cinnamon

2 large eggs, at room temperature

½ cup (72 g) brown sugar

½ cup (96 g) organic granulated sugar

½ cup (143 g) full-fat plain Greek yogurt

½ cup (120 ml) melted coconut oil

1 tsp pure vanilla extract

3 medium overripe bananas, mashed

Preheat the oven to 350°F (177°C) and grease and line a 9 x 5-inch (23 x 13-cm) loaf pan.

In a large bowl, mix together the whole-wheat pastry flour, oat flour, baking soda, salt, nutmeg and cinnamon. Set the bowl aside.

In another large bowl, whisk together the eggs, brown sugar and granulated sugar. Mix in the yogurt, oil and vanilla. Fold in the bananas.

Pour the banana-yogurt mixture into the flour mixture and stir until the mixtures are just combined. Do not overmix or the bread may become tough.

Allow the batter to rest for 10 minutes. Pour the batter into the greased loaf pan. Bake for about 60 minutes, or until a toothpick comes out clean from the center.

Allow the banana bread to cool before serving.

Notes: If you cannot find whole-wheat pastry flour, you can substitute it one-to-one with white whole-wheat flour.

For optional decoration, peel and slice another whole banana, lengthwise. Gently arrange the banana on top, interior side up.

Extra Swap: I used Greek yogurt and coconut oil instead of canola oil and butter. These healthy fats keep the bread light and moist while also adding extra protein.

CHICKPEA-OATMEAL COOKIE DOUGH TRUFFLES

Chickpeas are growing in popularity and not just for savory dishes. Their creamy texture and delicate flavor make them great in desserts as well. Chickpeas serve as the star ingredient in this delicious, wholesome treat. The chickpeas' texture, when blended with peanut butter, maple syrup, brown sugar and oats, perfectly mimics the texture of cookie dough. Coated in rich dark chocolate, these truffles make for one irresistible dessert!

YIELD: 16 TO 18 TRUFFLES

1 (15-oz [425-g]) can chickpeas, drained, rinsed and patted dry with a paper towel (see Notes)

½ cup (130 g) peanut butter or almond butter (see Notes)

½ tsp salt

1½ tsp (5 g) ground cinnamon

2½ tbsp (23 g) brown sugar or coconut sugar

2 tbsp (30 ml) pure maple syrup

2 tsp (10 ml) pure vanilla extract

½ cup (40 g) rolled oats

1½ cups (270 g) mini dark chocolate chips, divided

1 tbsp (15 g) coconut oil

Line a medium baking sheet with parchment paper.

In a food processor, combine the chickpeas, peanut butter, salt, cinnamon, brown sugar, maple syrup and vanilla. Process the ingredients until they form a thick, sticky paste. Add the oats and pulse until the oats are broken down and incorporated throughout the cookie dough mixture. Transfer the cookie dough to a medium bowl.

Gently fold ½ cup (90 g) of the chocolate chips into the cookie dough.

Using a 1-tablespoon (15-g) measuring spoon or cookie scoop, scoop out some of the cookie dough and form it into a small ball. Place the ball on the prepared baking sheet. Continue this process until all of the cookie dough is used—it should create 16 to 18 balls. Place the baking sheet in the freezer for 10 to 15 minutes, until the cookie dough balls are set and slightly hardened.

Meanwhile, place the remaining 1 cup (180 g) of chocolate chips and oil in a small microwave-safe bowl and microwave them at 50 percent power in 45-second increments, stirring the chocolate between each increment, until the chocolate is fully melted and smooth.

Using a fork, dip each cookie dough ball into the melted chocolate to completely coat the cookie dough. Return the cookie dough ball to the baking sheet. Freeze the truffles for 10 to 15 minutes, or until the chocolate has hardened. The cookie dough truffles are best stored in an airtight container in the refrigerator.

Notes: Make sure the chickpeas are completely dry, so they do not add extra moisture to the cookie dough mixture; otherwise, the mixture will be too wet.

Make sure the nut butter is not too runny, or it will make the dough runny. I like to use Jif Natural Peanut Butter or Justin's brand peanut or almond butter.

Extra Swap: I coated these truffles in antioxidant-rich and low-sugar dark chocolate.

GLUTEN-FREE CHOCOLATE AND CITRUS OLIVE OIL CAKE

There is nothing better than rich, decadent chocolate cake. In my opinion, the perfect chocolate cake needs to be super chocolatey, balanced in flavor and sweetness, perfectly moist and covered in a creamy frosting. This gluten-free chocolate citrus and olive oil cake checks all those boxes. Olive oil gives this cake a light texture while also keeping it incredibly moist. I use a blood orange olive oil (which you can find at almost any artisan olive oil store or online) because its floral, citrusy notes balances and complements the intensity of the chocolate. For even more orange flavor, I use the zest of three oranges! The cake is also covered in a rich, fudge-like glaze that provides more chocolate flavor while also keeping the cake moist.

YIELD: 12 SERVINGS

Cake

½ cup (45 g) oat flour

¾ cup (72 g) almond flour

½ cup (48 g) cocoa powder

¾ tsp salt

¼ tsp freshly grated nutmeg

1 tsp instant espresso powder (optional)

½ tsp baking soda

1 cup (200 g) organic granulated sugar

1½ tbsp (9 g) orange zest

3 large eggs, at room temperature

¾ cup (180 ml) blood orange olive oil

1 tsp pure vanilla extract

¼ cup (60 ml) boiling water

Thin orange slices (such as a mixture of navel, cara cara and blood oranges), as needed

Chocolate Glaze

1 cup (120 g) powdered sugar

3 tbsp (18 g) cocoa powder

1 tsp agave

1 tsp pure vanilla extract

2½ tbsp (38 ml) unsweetened plain almond milk or cashew milk

Pinch of salt

To make the cake, preheat the oven to 325°F (163°C). Grease a 9-inch (23-cm) round cake pan, then line it with parchment paper.

In a medium bowl, whisk together the oat flour, almond flour, cocoa powder, salt, nutmeg, espresso powder (if using) and baking soda. Set the flour mixture aside.

In another medium bowl, combine the granulated sugar and orange zest. Gently massage the orange zest with the sugar, so that the zest releases its natural oils and becomes floral. Add the eggs, one at a time, to the sugar mixture and beat each egg until it is well combined with the sugar mixture. Whisk in the oil and vanilla. Slowly add the oil mixture to the flour mixture and mix until they are just combined.

Add the water and stir until everything is well incorporated. Do not overmix the batter. Pour the batter into the prepared cake pan.

Bake the cake for 30 to 35 minutes, until a toothpick inserted into the center comes out clean. Allow the cake to cool completely.

Meanwhile, make the chocolate glaze. In a small bowl, whisk together the powdered sugar, cocoa powder, agave, vanilla, almond milk and salt. Pour the glaze over the cooled cake and spread it with a spatula or spoon until it evenly covers the top of the cake.

Top the glazed cake with the orange slices.

Extra Swap: The cake swaps canola oil with olive oil, which is rich in healthy monounsaturated fats and antioxidants.

HEALTHY LEMON BARS

These lemon bars have a crumbly, tender shortbread crust and a bright, creamy, perfectly sweet lemon curd. You would never guess these lemon bars are gluten-free and dairy-free. The buttery, nutty shortbread crust is made with coconut oil, almond flour and coconut flour, while the light lemon filling is made with just four simple ingredients: fresh lemon, organic granulated sugar, eggs and coconut flour. It's a sweet and tart treat that you will love!

YIELD: 9 BARS

Crust

1½ cups (144 g) superfine almond flour (such as Bob's Red Mill brand)

½ cup (56 g) coconut flour

½ tsp salt

¼ cup (60 ml) pure maple syrup

¼ cup (60 ml) melted coconut oil

½ tsp pure vanilla extract

Filling

½ cup (96 g) organic granulated sugar

2 tbsp (14 g) coconut flour, sifted

4 large eggs, at room temperature

1 large egg yolk, at room temperature

½ cup (120 ml) fresh lemon juice, at room temperature

Zest of 1 medium lemon

Topping

½ cup (60 g) powdered sugar

To make the crust, preheat the oven to 350°F (177°C). Grease an 8 x 8-inch (20 x 20-cm) baking pan, then line it with parchment paper.

In a large bowl, mix together the almond flour, coconut flour and salt. Add the maple syrup, oil and vanilla and mix until a wet dough forms; you should be able to form the dough into a ball.

Transfer the dough to the baking pan and spread it out evenly on the bottom of the pan. Bake the crust for 16 to 22 minutes, or until golden brown.

While the crust bakes, make the filling by combining the sugar and coconut flour in a large bowl. Add the eggs and egg yolk and whisk to combine the ingredients.

Slowly add the lemon juice, stirring constantly until the filling is smooth. Gently fold in the lemon zest.

As soon as you remove the crust from the oven, pour the filling over the hot crust. This step is crucial as it helps prevent a soggy crust. The filling will be slightly runny, but it will firm up as it bakes.

Reduce the oven's temperature to 325°F (163°C).

Bake the lemon bars for 22 to 25 minutes, until the filling is set in the middle and does not jiggle. Turn off the oven and slightly open the oven door. Allow the bars to sit in the oven for 10 minutes.

Remove the lemon bars from the oven and allow them to cool. Transfer them to the refrigerator for at least 4 hours to fully set before slicing. Once set, cut into 9 squares and top each with powdered sugar.

Note: If the lemon bars crack, do not fret! Just cover them with powdered sugar and enjoy. They will still taste amazing!

SPECTACULAR SUPPERS *and* SNACKS USING HEALTHY FATS

The Swap: Unprocessed and healthy natural fats instead of nutrient-void and caloric fats.

....

This chapter will introduce you to healthier fat options. Healthy fat is essential for our bodies, as it boosts brain function, lowers cholesterol and helps us feel full and satisfied. The key for finding healthy fats is to look for ingredients that are unprocessed and naturally high in fats. Some of my favorites are Greek yogurt, avocado, cottage cheese, pumpkin, olive oil and coconut oil—these items take the place of things like mayo, cream cheese, vegetable oil, sour cream or high-fat dairy milk.

My favorite fat swap ingredient to use is Greek yogurt. There are several reasons I love it so much. First, Greek yogurt is a nutrient-packed ingredient that boasts many health benefits. It's full of protein to keep you full and strong, probiotics to boost your immune system and decrease stomach issues, calcium to keep your muscles and vital organs functioning and potassium to help lower your blood pressure and balance the sodium levels in your body. It also has a creamy texture and mild, slightly tangy taste that makes it a great substitute for unhealthy fat sources. Greek yogurt can be used in many different applications, like in my Buffalo Chicken Pasta Bake (page 66) or Vanilla Bean and Cinnamon French Toast Bake with Mixed Berry Sauce (page 77). It's a miracle ingredient!

Avocado is an incredibly nutritious food with plenty of healthy fat and nutrients. This fruit offers approximately 20 vitamins, minerals and antioxidants, including vitamins K, C, E and B6, as well as potassium and lutein. It's delicious on toast, tossed in a salad or blended into creamy dressings, like the Avocado Ranch on page 62. Avocado can also be the perfect condiment—try it in my Chicken Caprese Paninis with Avocado-Basil Aioli (page 73).

Cottage cheese, with its creamy texture and mild flavor, is a versatile ingredient in the kitchen for both sweet and savory recipes. Cottage cheese is healthy to eat as part of a balanced diet because it's low in fat and sodium and serves as a source of several essential nutrients. It provides lusciousness while vastly reducing the fat in my Healthier New York–Style Cheesecake with Macerated Strawberries (page 79).

Pumpkin is also a great fat substitute. It's extremely popular in the fall for so many recipes, but it's actually something that can and should be enjoyed year-round for its wonderful health benefits. It's packed with vitamin A, potassium and antioxidants and is low in fat and calories. It also has a wonderful taste and creamy texture that makes it a star in my Chai-Spiced Pumpkin Waffles with Greek Yogurt Cream Cheese Glaze (page 83).

Extra virgin olive oil is the main oil I use for cooking. I also love to use it in dressings and sauces, and I enjoy using a drizzle to add the finishing touch to a dish. Good-quality olive oil contains essential vitamins, nutrients and antioxidants and is gentle on your digestive system. I call for extra virgin olive oil in several of the recipes in this chapter, including two tasty dinner options: Chicken Caesar Salad with Whole-Wheat Croutons and Greek Yogurt Dressing (page 69) and Brussels and Bacon Pasta Carbonara (page 74).

Coconut oil is the second most used oil in my house. It's been shown to help combat high blood pressure, it's thought to help energy levels and boost your metabolism and it may aid in lowering inflammation. It has a beautiful light coconut flavor, which makes my Coconut Shrimp with Mango-Chili Sauce (page 61) irresistible!

GREEK YOGURT BEEF STROGANOFF

My father taught me how to make beef stroganoff. He taught me the basic recipe and I gave it a healthy Danilicious twist. I lightened the dish by replacing the sour cream with protein-rich Greek yogurt. Greek yogurt and sour cream are nearly identical in flavor, but Greek yogurt contains many more nutrients. That's why it's one of my favorite—and easiest—swaps. This dish is just as homey, comforting and delicious as the traditional version. In fact, after one bite, my dad admitted it was even better than his recipe, and he couldn't even tell it was made healthier!

YIELD: 4 TO 6 SERVINGS

1 lb (454 g) filet mignon or sirloin steak, cut into thin strips

1½ tsp (8 g) salt, divided

½ tsp black pepper, divided

2½ tbsp (38 ml) extra virgin olive oil, divided

1 small onion, thinly sliced

1½ cups (99 g) thinly sliced cremini or button mushrooms

4 to 5 cloves garlic, minced

2 tbsp (16 g) white whole-wheat flour

1½ cups (360 ml) beef broth

⅛ tsp ground nutmeg

½ tsp dried thyme

½ tsp mustard powder

2 tsp (10 g) Dijon mustard

2 tsp (10 ml) Worcestershire sauce

½ cup (143 g) plain Greek yogurt, at room temperature

2 tbsp (30 ml) cream sherry (optional)

¼ cup (36 g) capers (optional)

6 oz (170 g) cooked egg noodles

1 tbsp (3 g) finely chopped fresh parsley (optional)

Season the steak with 1 teaspoon of the salt and ¼ teaspoon of the black pepper.

In a large sauté pan, heat 1 tablespoon (15 ml) of the oil over medium-high heat. Add the steak to the sauté pan in batches so as to not overcrowd the pan. Cook the steak for about 2 minutes per side, until it forms a golden-brown crust but is still pink in the middle. Remove the steak from the sauté pan and set it aside.

Set the sauté pan over medium heat and add 1 tablespoon (15 ml) of the oil. Add the onion and mushrooms and cook them for 4 to 5 minutes, until they are browned and caramelized. Add the garlic and sauté the mixture for 1 minute.

Add the remaining ½ tablespoon (8 ml) of oil and flour to the onion mixture. Cook the mixture for 1 minute. Slowly add the broth, whisking the mixture constantly to thoroughly incorporate the broth. Add the remaining ½ teaspoon of salt, remaining ¼ teaspoon of black pepper, nutmeg, thyme and mustard powder. Cook the mixture for about 5 minutes, stirring often, until it begins to thicken.

Add the Dijon mustard, Worcestershire sauce, yogurt and cream sherry (if using) and stir until the ingredients are well combined. Reduce the heat to medium-low and bring the sauce to a gentle simmer. Cook the sauce for 1 to 2 minutes, until it thickens slightly and the yogurt is completely melted.

Add the beef and its juices and the capers (if using). Simmer the sauce for 1 minute, then remove it from the heat immediately. Taste it and adjust the seasonings as desired.

Serve the sauce over the egg noodles, garnished with the parsley (if using).

Extra Swap: I amped up the flavor by using a few more spices than my dad's recipe calls for. Spices are a great way to add flavor without adding calories or fat. You can also serve the beef stroganoff over my Roasted Garlic and Cream Cheese Mashed Cauliflower (page 109) for a low-carb option.

COCONUT SHRIMP WITH MANGO-CHILI SAUCE

This is a healthier take on a beloved tropical appetizer. Plump Gulf shrimp are double coated in crispy panko breadcrumbs and sweet shredded coconut, then they are lightly fried to crispy perfection in coconut oil. Coconut oil helps reinforce the beautiful coconut flavor while also adding nutrients to the dish. The delicious shrimp is then dipped in a sweet and spicy mango-chili sauce. This recipe is sure to be a huge hit at your next get-together!

YIELD: 20 TO 25 SERVINGS

Mango-Chili Sauce

1 cup (165 g) frozen or fresh cubed mango

1½ tbsp (23 ml) water

2 tbsp (30 ml) sweet chili sauce (such as Sky Valley brand)

2 tsp (10 ml) honey

1 tsp apple cider vinegar

1 tsp minced ginger

2 tsp (6 g) minced garlic

½ tsp salt

Coconut Shrimp

⅓ cup (43 g) white whole-wheat flour

1 tsp salt, divided, plus more as needed

1 tsp garlic powder

½ tsp paprika

¼ tsp cayenne pepper

3 large eggs

1½ tbsp (23 ml) water

1¼ cups (112 g) whole-wheat panko breadcrumbs

2 cups (152 g) sweetened shredded coconut

20 to 25 jumbo Gulf shrimp, deveined and patted dry

1 cup (240 g) coconut oil

To make the mango-chili sauce, combine the mango, water, sweet chili sauce, honey, vinegar, ginger, garlic and salt in a medium saucepan over medium heat. Bring the mixture to a gentle boil. Reduce the heat to medium-low and simmer the mixture for 6 to 8 minutes, until the mango is soft and the liquid has thickened slightly. Transfer the mixture to a small food processor or blender and process until the sauce is smooth but still thick. Set the sauce aside.

To make the coconut shrimp, set out three wide, shallow bowls to create a breading station. Set a large baking sheet next to the breading station. In the first bowl, combine the flour, ½ teaspoon of the salt, garlic powder, paprika and cayenne pepper. In the second bowl, whisk together the eggs and water. In the third bowl, combine the breadcrumbs, coconut and remaining ½ teaspoon of salt.

Coat each shrimp with the flour mixture, then the egg mixture and finally the breadcrumb-coconut mixture, placing each breaded shrimp on the baking sheet. Dip each shrimp back into the egg mixture and then into the breadcrumb-coconut mixture for a second coating. Allow the breaded shrimp to rest for 30 minutes, so that the coating will properly adhere.

In a deep Dutch oven or pot, heat the oil to 350°F (177°C). If you do not have a thermometer to monitor the oil's temperature, you can test it by adding a few breadcrumbs to the oil. If they sizzle and pop, the oil is hot enough.

While the oil is heating, line another large baking sheet or a large platter with paper towels. Set this baking sheet within arm's reach of the Dutch oven.

Add the coconut shrimp to the oil in batches so as to not overcrowd the Dutch oven. Cook the shrimp for 3 to 4 minutes per side, or until they are cooked through and their internal temperature reaches 145°F (63°C). Place the fried shrimp on the prepared baking sheet to soak up any extra oil and sprinkle the shrimp with additional salt.

Serve the shrimp with the mango-chili sauce for dipping.

Extra Swap: The sauce is sweetened with only honey and the natural sweetness from the mango.

COBB SALAD WITH AVOCADO RANCH

A Cobb salad often seems like a healthy lunch option but can actually be just as bad for you as a burger. The problem is the heavy ranch that dresses the salad. Which is sad, I know, because a Cobb salad served with a great ranch is the best! That's why I created a healthier version topped with a luscious, flavor-packed, herbaceous avocado ranch. Avocado provides a silky texture to the dressing while also adding healthy fat and nutrients. The salad still has all the classic goodies, like chicken, bacon, cheese, tomatoes, avocado and hard-boiled eggs. This salad is the perfect healthy lunch option!

YIELD: 6 TO 8 SERVINGS

....

Avocado Ranch

1 large avocado

Juice of 1 medium lemon

2 green onions (white parts only)

¼ cup (12 g) fresh cilantro

¼ cup (15 g) fresh parsley

4 to 5 large leaves fresh basil

3 tbsp (45 ml) extra virgin olive oil

½ tsp salt

1 tsp Worcestershire sauce

¼ tsp agave

2 to 3 cloves garlic

2 to 4 tbsp (30 to 60 ml) water

Cobb Salad

4 to 5 cups (188 to 235 g) coarsely chopped romaine lettuce

1 cup (140 g) cubed cooked chicken (see Note)

½ cup (56 g) crumbled cooked bacon

½ cup (83 g) halved cherry tomatoes

½ cup (56 g) crumbled herbed goat cheese or blue cheese

1 large avocado, thinly sliced

½ cup (65 g) pickled red onions (page 93)

2 large hard-boiled eggs, thinly sliced

⅓ cup (36 g) roasted sliced almonds

To make the avocado ranch, combine the avocado, lemon juice, green onions, cilantro, parsley, basil, oil, salt, Worcestershire sauce, agave and garlic in a small food processor. Process until the ingredients are smooth. Add the water, 1 tablespoon (15 ml) at a time, until you reach your desired consistency. Set the dressing aside.

To make the Cobb salad, place the lettuce in a large salad bowl. Top the lettuce with the chicken, bacon, tomatoes, goat cheese, avocado, pickled red onions, eggs and almonds. Dress the salad with the desired amount of avocado ranch dressing. Toss the salad to thoroughly dress it.

....

Note: To make this salad even easier to prepare, I buy a rotisserie chicken and cut the meat into cubes.

LOADED GREEK YOGURT CHICKEN SALAD

This chicken salad is bursting with flavor and texture and made healthier with Greek yogurt. Chicken salad is usually drenched in mayo, which is high in fat and low in nutritional value. I replaced most of the mayo in the dressing with protein-rich Greek yogurt and combined it with other bright flavors like honey, fresh lemon juice and Dijon mustard. The salad is also loaded with grapes for juicy sweetness, green apples for a tart crunch, dried cranberries for a touch of tartness and pecans for that salty, nutty bite. It's an explosion of flavor, and you would never guess it is healthy.

YIELD: 4 TO 6 SERVINGS

Dressing

½ cup (143 g) plain Greek yogurt

2½ tbsp (35 g) olive oil mayo

1½ tsp (8 g) Dijon mustard

1½ tbsp (23 ml) fresh lemon juice

1½ tbsp (23 ml) honey

1 tsp Worcestershire sauce

1 tsp apple cider vinegar

½ tsp garlic powder

¼ tsp onion powder

½ tsp celery salt

Chicken Salad

3 cups (405 g) shredded cooked chicken breast (see Note)

½ cup (51 g) diced celery

½ cup (76 g) halved red seedless grapes

½ cup (61 g) coarsely chopped roasted salted pecans or walnuts

¼ cup (30 g) dried cranberries

½ cup (63 g) diced green apple

¼ cup (38 g) diced red onion

Salt, as needed

Black pepper, as needed

2 tbsp (6 g) finely chopped celery leaves or fresh parsley

For Serving

4 to 6 slices toasted whole-wheat bread

1 large avocado, thinly sliced

To make the dressing, combine the yogurt, mayo, mustard, lemon juice, honey, Worcestershire sauce, vinegar, garlic powder, onion powder and celery salt in a large bowl.

To make the chicken salad, add the chicken, celery, grapes, pecans, cranberries, apple, onion, salt and black pepper to the bowl of dressing. Stir the mixture until all of the ingredients are coated in the dressing. Taste the chicken salad and adjust the seasonings if needed.

Refrigerate the chicken salad for at least 1 hour. Remove it from the refrigerator just prior to serving, and then garnish it with the celery leaves.

To serve the chicken salad, place it on top of the slices of bread and top the chicken salad with the avocado.

Note: If you're looking for a shortcut, try shredding a rotisserie chicken breast!

Extra Swaps: The dressing is only sweetened with unrefined honey. Plus, I serve the chicken salad on whole-wheat toast to add extra fiber and nutrients.

BUFFALO CHICKEN PASTA BAKE

This is everything you love about Buffalo chicken dip in a healthy, easy, delicious weeknight meal! It's a combination of gluten-free penne pasta, roasted chicken, sautéed veggies and a creamy, spicy Greek yogurt Buffalo sauce. The mixture is then topped with a Greek yogurt ranch and cheese and baked to perfection. Greek yogurt helps lighten up this dish by replacing most of the butter in the sauce and mayo in the ranch while still leaving the final product creamy and delicious. This pasta bake is my little brother's new obsession, who says it's his favorite dish in the book.

YIELD: 10 TO 12 SERVINGS

1 (8-oz [227-g]) package gluten-free penne pasta (such as Banza brand)

1 tbsp (15 ml) extra virgin olive oil

2 large carrots, diced

2 large ribs celery, diced

½ small red onion, diced

3 to 4 cloves garlic, finely chopped

½ tsp salt

Pinch of black pepper

⅓ to ½ cup (80 to 120 ml) hot sauce (such as Frank's RedHot® brand)

½ cup (120 ml) chicken broth

2 tbsp (30 g) butter

¾ cup (214 g) plain Greek yogurt, divided

2 cups (270 g) shredded cooked chicken (see Note)

¾ cup (180 ml) Greek yogurt ranch dressing (such as Bolthouse Farms brand), divided

1 cup (112 g) shredded mozzarella cheese

¾ cup (90 g) shredded Cheddar cheese

2 tbsp (8 g) chopped parsley (optional)

Preheat the oven to 375°F (191°C). Grease a 13 x 7–inch (33 x 18–cm) baking dish.

Cook the pasta according to the package's instructions. Set the pasta aside.

In a large pot, heat the oil over medium heat. Add the carrots, celery and onion. Cook the vegetables for 3 to 5 minutes, until they are tender. Add the garlic, salt and black pepper, and cook the mixture for 1 to 2 minutes, or until the garlic is fragrant. Remove the mixture from the pot.

Add the hot sauce, broth, butter and ½ cup (143 g) of the Greek yogurt to the pot and stir until the ingredients are well combined and the butter is fully melted. Add the vegetable mixture, chicken and pasta and stir until all of the ingredients are coated in the sauce. Add the remaining ¼ cup (71 g) of Greek yogurt and stir until the mixture is creamy and thoroughly combined.

Transfer the pasta to the prepared baking dish. Top the pasta with ½ cup (120 ml) of the ranch dressing, the mozzarella cheese and the Cheddar cheese. Bake the pasta for 12 to 15 minutes, or until the cheeses are melted and golden brown.

Garnish the pasta bake with the parsley and remaining ¼ cup (60 ml) of ranch dressing, if using.

Note: To make this recipe even easier, shred a rotisserie chicken!

Extra Swap: I use a gluten-free pasta, which adds fiber and nutrients. Plus, it is easier on digestion than regular starchy pasta!

CHICKEN CAESAR SALAD WITH WHOLE-WHEAT CROUTONS AND GREEK YOGURT DRESSING

This salad is a healthier take on Caesar salad! The dressing is lightened by using a base of Greek yogurt instead of heavy mayo. The Greek yogurt is flavored with punchy garlic, salty grated Parmesan cheese, bright lemon juice and umami-packed miso. The salad contains all the classic fixings of traditional Caesar salad: romaine lettuce, shaved Parmesan and chicken. Finally, crunchy, perfectly seasoned homemade whole-wheat croutons adorn the top of the salad.

YIELD: 6 TO 10 SERVINGS

Whole-Wheat Croutons

3 tbsp (45 ml) extra virgin olive oil

1 tsp Worcestershire sauce

1 tsp Italian seasoning

½ tsp garlic powder

½ tsp salt

¼ tsp black pepper

2 cups (70 g) cubed whole-wheat French bread

Greek Yogurt Caesar Dressing

½ cup (143 g) plain Greek yogurt

2 tbsp (30 ml) unsweetened plain almond milk or cashew milk

2 tbsp (30 ml) extra virgin olive oil

2 tsp (12 g) white miso paste

2½ tsp (13 ml) Worcestershire sauce

3 tbsp (45 ml) fresh lemon juice

2 to 3 cloves garlic, minced

2 tsp (10 g) Dijon mustard

½ tsp salt

Pinch of black pepper

¼ cup (45 g) grated fresh Parmesan cheese

Chicken Caesar Salad

1 large head romaine lettuce, coarsely chopped

1 cup (140 g) cubed cooked chicken (see Notes)

¾ cup (84 g) shaved fresh Parmesan cheese

To make the whole-wheat croutons, preheat the oven to 400°F (204°C). Lightly grease a large baking sheet.

In a large bowl, mix together the oil, Worcestershire sauce, Italian seasoning, garlic powder, salt and black pepper. Add the cubed bread and toss, so that all of the bread is coated in the oil mixture. Spread the bread out on the prepared baking sheet. Bake the croutons for 12 to 15 minutes, stirring them halfway through the baking time, until the croutons are golden brown and crunchy. Allow the croutons to cool completely.

To make the Greek yogurt Caesar dressing, combine the yogurt, almond milk, oil, miso paste, Worcestershire sauce, lemon juice, garlic, mustard, salt and black pepper in a large bowl. Whisk the ingredients until the dressing is smooth. Gently fold the Parmesan cheese into the dressing.

To make the chicken Caesar salad, place the lettuce in a large salad bowl. Top the lettuce with 1 cup (35 g) of the croutons, the chicken, Parmesan cheese and ½ to 1 cup (120 to 240 ml) of the dressing. Toss the salad until all of the ingredients are well combined.

Notes: To make this recipe even easier, shred a rotisserie chicken!

Store extra dressing in an airtight container in the refrigerator for up to 1 week. Store extra croutons in an airtight container for up to 2 weeks.

Extra Swap: I use whole-wheat bread for the croutons instead of regular white bread to add fiber and nutrients.

CARAMELIZED ONION DIP WITH ROASTED VEGGIE CHIPS

This is a fresh, more delicious and healthier take on classic French onion dip and chips. The onion dip is made more flavorful by employing slowly caramelized onions. Caramelizing the onions gives them a sweeter, bolder taste that makes this dip irresistible. The dip is also made healthier by replacing most of the usual mayo with Greek yogurt.

YIELD: 8 TO 10 SERVINGS

Caramelized Onion Dip

1 to 3 tsp (5 to 15 ml) extra virgin olive oil, divided

1 large onion, diced

2 to 3 cloves garlic, minced

1 tbsp (15 ml) Worcestershire sauce

¾ tsp salt, divided

½ tsp garlic powder

½ tsp onion powder

¾ cup (214 g) plain Greek yogurt

⅓ cup (73 g) olive oil mayo

¼ tsp Hungarian hot paprika or cayenne pepper

¼ tsp black pepper

1 tbsp (3 g) finely chopped fresh parsley

Roasted Veggie Chips

1 large sweet potato, cut into thin chips

2 small beets, cut into thin chips

2 large red potatoes, cut into thin chips

1 to 2 tbsp (15 to 30 ml) extra virgin olive oil

1 tsp garlic powder

½ tsp black pepper

½ tsp salt

To make the caramelized onion dip, heat 1 teaspoon of the oil in a large skillet over medium-low heat. Add the onion and cook it for 25 to 30 minutes, stirring occasionally, until the onion is tender and golden brown. If the skillet becomes too dry during cooking, add more of the oil, so that the onions do not burn.

Add the garlic and cook the mixture for 2 to 3 minutes, until the garlic is fragrant. Add the Worcestershire sauce and ½ teaspoon of the salt, stirring to combine the ingredients. Remove the skillet from the heat and allow the onion mixture to cool completely.

In a medium bowl, mix together the garlic powder, onion powder, Greek yogurt, mayo, Hungarian hot paprika, remaining ¼ teaspoon of salt and black pepper. Stir in the caramelized onions. Top the dip with the parsley. Place the dip in the refrigerator to chill until you are ready to serve it.

To make the roasted veggie chips, soak the sweet potato chips, beet chips and red potato chips in cold water for 30 minutes to remove excess starch. Dry the chips completely with paper towels.

Preheat the oven to 375°F (191°C). Lightly grease a large baking sheet.

In a large bowl, combine the veggie chips, 1 tablespoon (15 ml) of the oil, garlic powder, black pepper and salt. Stir the chips to fully coat them with the oil and seasonings. If the chips seem dry, add the remaining 1 tablespoon (15 ml) of oil.

Spread out the chips on the prepared baking sheet. Bake the chips for 15 to 20 minutes, flipping them halfway through the baking time, until they are golden brown and crispy. Note that sometimes the chips on the outer edges of the baking sheet cook more quickly. If this happens, remove those chips when they are golden brown and continue cooking the rest of the chips until they are fully baked.

Serve the caramelized onion dip with the roasted veggie chips.

Extra Swap: The dip is served with crispy baked—not fried—root veggie chips.

CHICKEN CAPRESE PANINIS WITH AVOCADO-BASIL AIOLI

My hubby and I are sandwich lovers—we especially adore warm, gooey, crunchy paninis. This panini recipe is one of our absolute favorites. Whole-grain bread is topped with deli-sliced chicken, fresh mozzarella, juicy tomatoes and an incredibly delicious avocado-basil aioli. The avocado replaces the mayo and creates a creamy, flavor-packed sauce, which is what makes this sandwich so good! This panini takes classic caprese flavors to a whole new level!

YIELD: 4 SERVINGS

Avocado-Basil Aioli

¼ cup (30 g) raw walnuts

3 tbsp (45 ml) fresh lemon juice

2 to 3 cloves garlic

1 cup (16 g) fresh basil leaves

1 large avocado

½ tsp salt

1 tbsp (15 ml) water

Paninis

1 to 2 tbsp (15 to 30 ml) extra virgin olive oil, plus more as needed

8 slices whole-wheat bread

8 oz (227 g) fresh mozzarella cheese, thinly sliced (see Note)

3 to 4 medium Roma tomatoes, thinly sliced

8 oz (227 g) thinly sliced deli chicken

8 leaves fresh basil

Olive oil, for drizzling, plus more if needed

½ tsp garlic salt

To make the avocado-basil aioli, combine the walnuts, lemon juice, garlic, basil, avocado, salt and water in a small food processor. Process the ingredients for 1 to 2 minutes, until the aioli is smooth and thick.

To make the paninis, preheat the panini press on medium heat. Lightly grease the panini press with the oil.

Smear the aioli on each slice of bread. Top 4 slices of bread with slices of mozzarella cheese, the tomatoes, the chicken and the basil. Top the sandwiches with the other 4 slices of bread, aioli side down. Drizzle each slice of bread with oil and sprinkle each slice with the garlic salt.

Add the paninis to the panini press, cooking them in batches if necessary. Cook the paninis on medium for 4 to 6 minutes, or until the bread is golden brown and the cheese is melted. If you don't have a panini press, heat ½ tablespoon (8 ml) of olive oil in a large skillet over medium heat and cook the sandwiches for 3 to 4 minutes per side, or until the bread is golden brown and the cheese is melted.

Slice the paninis in half and serve.

Note: I recommend taking the cheese out of the refrigerator 30 minutes prior to cooking the sandwiches, so that the cheese melts better.

Extra Swap: I use whole-wheat bread instead of white bread to add fiber and extra nutrients.

BRUSSELS AND BACON PASTA CARBONARA

This recipe mashes up two of my favorites: pasta carbonara and bacon-balsamic Brussels sprouts. The result is a simple, healthy and crazy-flavorful meal! To lighten it up, I replaced some of the eggs with Greek yogurt, which creates a creamy and rich sauce. I also used a gluten-free brown rice thin spaghetti, which contains fiber and protein. Finally, I added Brussels sprouts for some vegetable goodness. This pasta is a weeknight staple in my house!

YIELD: 4 TO 6 SERVINGS

8 oz (227 g) gluten-free brown rice thin spaghetti (I like Jovial)

2 large eggs, at room temperature

3 tbsp (54 g) plain Greek yogurt, at room temperature

¾ cup (135 g) grated Parmesan cheese, divided

½ tsp salt

¼ tsp black pepper, plus more as needed

4 to 5 slices thick-cut bacon

½ tbsp (8 ml) extra virgin olive oil

2 cups (226 g) shredded Brussels sprouts

4 to 5 cloves garlic, minced

1 tbsp (6 g) lemon zest

1 tbsp (15 ml) lemon juice

1 to 2 tbsp (15 to 30 ml) balsamic vinegar glaze (see Note)

Cook the spaghetti according to the package's instructions, reserving 1 cup (240 ml) of the cooking water.

In a small bowl, mix together the eggs and yogurt until the mixture is smooth and creamy. Gently stir in ½ cup (90 g) of the Parmesan cheese, salt and black pepper. Set this mixture aside.

In a large skillet over medium heat, cook the bacon for 8 to 10 minutes, until the fat is rendered and the bacon is crispy. Remove the bacon from the skillet and chop the bacon into medium-sized pieces. Wipe out the skillet, leaving about 1 tablespoon (15 ml) of the bacon fat.

Add the oil to the skillet and return the skillet to medium heat. Add the Brussels sprouts and cook them for 4 to 6 minutes, until they are tender and slightly charred. Add the garlic and cook the mixture for 1 to 2 minutes, or until the garlic is fragrant. Be careful not to burn the garlic.

Add the spaghetti and bacon to the Brussels sprouts and stir to combine the ingredients. Remove the pasta from the heat.

Slowly stir in the egg mixture and toss it with the pasta mixture, so that the warmth of the pasta cooks the eggs and creates a creamy sauce. If the pasta seems too dry, add a little of the reserved pasta cooking water to help make it creamier.

Add the lemon zest and lemon juice and stir until everything is well combined. Taste and adjust seasonings as necessary.

Divide the pasta among four to six bowls. Drizzle each serving with the balsamic vinegar glaze. Top each serving with some of the remaining ¼ cup (45 g) of Parmesan cheese and additional black pepper.

Note: I recommend using Fini Modena balsamic vinegar glaze, as it has significantly less sugar than many other brands.

Extra Swap: I use brown rice gluten-free pasta in place of starchy white spaghetti to add extra protein and nutrients.

VANILLA BEAN AND CINNAMON FRENCH TOAST BAKE WITH MIXED BERRY SAUCE

This vanilla bean and cinnamon French toast bake takes breakfast to a whole new level: Pieces of multigrain bread are soaked in a creamy, vanilla bean custard, topped with cinnamon and sugar, baked to perfection and served with a tart and sweet berry sauce. Yum! Best yet, it's made without any heavy cream or high-fat milk. Instead, I use almond milk and Greek yogurt to create a luscious custard that is still light and nutritious. Greek yogurt mixed with almond milk is a great substitute for heavy cream because the combination is creamy but low in fat and high in protein. This crowd-pleasing, pretty dish is perfect for brunch with friends or breakfast at home with the family.

YIELD: 12 SERVINGS

French Toast Bake

1¾ cups (420 ml) unsweetened vanilla almond milk or cashew milk

½ cup (143 g) vanilla bean or vanilla Greek yogurt (I like Chobani or Siggi's)

6 large eggs, beaten

¼ cup (60 ml) pure maple syrup

¼ cup (36 g) plus 2 tsp (6 g) brown sugar, divided

2 tsp (10 g) vanilla bean paste

1 tsp ground cinnamon, divided

¼ tsp ground nutmeg

1 (12-oz [340-g]) whole-wheat or multigrain French baguette, cubed (see Note)

To make the French toast bake, preheat the oven to 375°F (191°C). Grease a 9 x 13–inch (23 x 33–cm) baking dish.

In a large bowl, whisk together the almond milk, yogurt, eggs, maple syrup, ¼ cup (36 g) of the brown sugar, vanilla bean paste, ½ teaspoon of the cinnamon and nutmeg until the ingredients are smooth and creamy. Add the cubed bread and mix well, so that the bread is fully coated in the custard base. Allow the bread to soak in the custard for at least 1 hour.

Pour the bread and custard into the prepared baking dish. In a small bowl, mix together the remaining 2 teaspoons (6 g) of brown sugar and the remaining ½ teaspoon of cinnamon. Sprinkle the cinnamon sugar on top of the French toast mixture.

Bake the French toast for 35 to 40 minutes, or until the custard is set and the top is golden brown.

(Continued)

Mixed Berry Sauce

2 cups (296 g) frozen mixed berries

¼ cup (48 g) organic granulated sugar

2 tbsp (30 ml) pure maple syrup

2 tbsp (30 ml) fresh lemon juice

⅛ tsp salt

¼ cup (60 ml) lukewarm water

1½ tsp (5 g) cornstarch

1 tbsp (15 ml) cold water

While the French toast bakes, make the mixed berry sauce. In a medium saucepan over medium heat, combine the berries, granulated sugar, maple syrup, lemon juice, salt and lukewarm water. Cook the berries for 6 to 8 minutes, until the granulated sugar is dissolved, the berries soften and the mixture comes to a low boil. Mash the berries as they cook to help them break down.

Reduce the heat to medium-low and bring the sauce mixture to a simmer.

In a small bowl, mix together the cornstarch and cold water, stirring the mixture until no lumps are present. Add the cornstarch slurry to the berry mixture and stir to thoroughly combine the slurry and berry mixture. Increase the heat to medium-high and bring the mixture to a boil. Cook the sauce for 3 to 5 minutes, until it thickens. Remove the sauce from the heat and allow it to cool slightly.

Place some of the French toast bake on each plate and top each serving with the desired amount of the mixed berry sauce.

Note: If you're wondering how many cups of cubed bread you'll need, a 12-ounce (340-g) baguette will yield about 5 cups (175 g) of bread cubes.

Extra Swap: I use multigrain bread instead of white bread to add fiber and nutrients.

HEALTHIER NEW YORK–STYLE CHEESECAKE WITH MACERATED STRAWBERRIES

I created this recipe for my mom—cheesecake is her favorite dessert. This cheesecake is as creamy, indulgent and rich as the original, but it's made lighter with a few simple swaps. I replace half of the cream cheese in the filling with mild cottage cheese and Greek yogurt, which are blended until they are smooth so that they're undetectable in the cheesecake. They also add more protein while significantly reducing the fat and calories in the cheesecake. I also replace the butter in the crust with coconut oil. The coconut oil still creates a tender, crumbly crust while adding health benefits and nutrients not found in butter. My mom was shocked at how good this cheesecake is and said that this recipe is a winner! If you're in a creative mood, try this cheesecake with my quick strawberry jam (page 142) or mixed berry sauce (page 78).

YIELD: 10 TO 12 SERVINGS

Crust

2 cups (180 g) honey graham cracker crumbs

¼ cup (48 g) organic granulated sugar

¼ tsp salt

½ cup (120 ml) melted coconut oil

Filling

1 cup (285 g) plain Greek yogurt, strained and at room temperature (see Note)

1 cup (230 g) low-fat cottage cheese, at room temperature

1 tbsp (15 ml) fresh lemon juice

3 tbsp (45 ml) honey

2 tsp (10 g) vanilla bean paste or 2 tsp (10 ml) pure vanilla extract

3 large eggs, at room temperature

2 (8-oz [227-g]) packages low-fat cream cheese, at room temperature

¾ cup (144 g) organic granulated sugar

1½ tbsp (14 g) cornstarch

To make the crust, preheat the oven to 350°F (177°C). Spray an 8-inch (20-cm) or 9-inch (23-cm) springform pan with cooking spray.

In a medium bowl, whisk together the graham cracker crumbs, sugar and salt. Add the oil and stir until all of the ingredients are well combined. The mixture will resemble wet, crumbly sand.

Transfer the mixture to the prepared springform pan and press it into the bottom and along the sides of the pan using a measuring cup. Bake the crust for 8 to 10 minutes, until it is a light golden-brown color.

Remove the crust from the oven and allow it to cool completely.

To make the filling, reduce the oven's temperature to 325°F (163°C).

In a food processor, combine the yogurt, cottage cheese, lemon juice, honey and vanilla bean paste. Process the ingredients for 1 to 2 minutes, until they are smooth. Add the eggs and process until the ingredients are just combined.

Add the cream cheese, sugar and cornstarch to the bowl of a stand mixer fitted with the whisk attachment. Mix the ingredients on low speed for 1 to 2 minutes, scraping down the sides of the bowl as needed, until the ingredients come together and form a smooth batter. Scrape down the sides of the bowl, then mix the ingredients on low speed for 20 seconds.

With the mixer running on low speed, add the yogurt–cottage cheese mixture to the cream cheese mixture in two batches. Mix them together until they are well combined, scraping down the sides of the bowl as needed.

Pour the batter into the cooled graham cracker crust.

(Continued)

Macerated Strawberries

1 cup (166 g) thinly sliced strawberries

1 tbsp (15 ml) honey, plus more as needed

Create a water bath by placing a large roasting pan or casserole dish on the bottom rack of the oven and carefully filling it with the boiling water.

Place the cheesecake on the oven rack above the water bath. Bake an 8-inch (20-cm) cheesecake for 1 hour and 10 minutes or a 9-inch (23-cm) cheesecake for 1 hour, or until the middle is just set and not jiggly.

Turn the oven off and crack open the oven door with the cheesecake still inside the oven. Leave it there for 30 to 45 minutes.

Remove the cheesecake from the oven and allow it to cool at room temperature for 30 to 45 minutes. Remove the sides of the springform pan and place the cheesecake in the refrigerator, uncovered, for at least 4 hours up or to overnight so it can fully set.

To make the macerated strawberries, combine the strawberries and honey in a small bowl 30 minutes prior to serving the cheesecake. Leave the strawberries to macerate until just prior to serving the cheesecake.

Cut the cheesecake into 10 to 12 slices. Top each serving with the macerated strawberries and additional honey.

Note: Greek yogurt needs to be strained for at least an hour (or even overnight) to remove extra liquid. Place the yogurt in a sieve with a bowl underneath and allow the extra liquid to seep out of the yogurt and into the bowl. Discard the liquid in the bowl and use the strained Greek yogurt left behind in the sieve.

CHAI-SPICED PUMPKIN WAFFLES WITH GREEK YOGURT CREAM CHEESE GLAZE

Waffles are the perfect treat for the weekend. Waffles are basically dessert for breakfast; what's not to love! These decadent, fall-inspired waffles are made guilt free by replacing some of the fat in the batter with pumpkin and coconut oil—both make the waffles light and fluffy while adding nutrients. The waffles are then drizzled with a tangy and perfectly sweet Greek yogurt cream cheese glaze, making them a warm, cozy and extra delicious breakfast treat!

YIELD: 4 TO 6 SERVINGS

. . . .

Chai-Spiced Pumpkin Waffles

1 cup (130 g) whole-wheat flour

½ cup (45 g) oat flour

½ tsp salt

1 tsp ground cinnamon

¼ tsp ground nutmeg

¼ tsp ground cardamom

¼ tsp ground cloves

½ tsp ground ginger

½ tsp ground allspice

1 tsp baking powder

½ tsp baking soda

2 large eggs, at room temperature

2 tbsp (30 ml) pure maple syrup

2 tbsp (24 g) coconut sugar or brown sugar

¾ cup (184 g) canned pumpkin

3 tbsp (45 ml) melted coconut oil, plus more as needed

1¼ cups (300 ml) unsweetened plain almond milk or cashew milk, at room temperature

1 tsp vanilla

¼ cup (30 g) coarsely chopped pecans

Cream Cheese Glaze

3 tbsp (45 g) whipped cream cheese

3 tbsp (54 g) plain Greek yogurt

3 tbsp (45 ml) pure maple syrup

1 tsp pure vanilla extract

Pinch of salt

To make the chai-spiced pumpkin waffles, whisk together the whole-wheat flour, oat flour, salt, cinnamon, nutmeg, cardamom, cloves, ginger, allspice, baking powder and baking soda in a large bowl. In another large bowl, whisk together the eggs, maple syrup, sugar, pumpkin, 3 tablespoons (45 ml) of the oil, almond milk and vanilla. Gently pour the egg mixture into the flour mixture and stir until a smooth batter forms. Allow the batter to rest for 10 minutes.

Meanwhile, make the cream cheese glaze. In a medium bowl, whisk together the cream cheese, yogurt, maple syrup, vanilla and salt until a smooth glaze forms.

Heat a waffle maker and coat it with the additional oil.

Pour some of the batter into the waffle maker and cook the waffle according to the waffle maker's directions and to your desired level of doneness.

Remove the waffle from the waffle maker.

Serve the waffles drizzled with the cream cheese glaze and topped with the pecans.

. . . .

Extra Swap: Instead of extra cream cheese in the glaze, I use Greek yogurt, which adds protein and lowers the fat content and calorie count but still makes the glaze creamy and delicious.

THE HEALTHY CARB MAGIC OF VEGGIES *and* WHOLE GRAINS

The Swap: Nutrient-rich whole-grain, high-fiber carbs instead of empty, refined carbs.

Let's talk about carbs. There are many fad diets that tell you to give up carbs. I disagree! Truth be told, carbs are an important part of a balanced diet. In fact, you need carbs to keep you energized throughout the day. On top of being your body's main source of energy, carbs are also full of other essential vitamins and nutrients. But not all carbs are created equal.

The best carbohydrates to consume are those that contain a high amount of fiber, such as fruits, vegetables and whole grains. It takes longer for your body to convert these carbs to glucose. They also supply you with the largest amount of nutrients. However, you want to avoid refined carbs, like white rice, white bread and items made with white flour, as your body quickly breaks down the glucose, leaving you with little energy and poor nutritional value.

This chapter will introduce you to some whole-grain, high-fiber, delicious carb options like quinoa, farro and brown rice. In the pages that follow, you will find amazing dishes like Hawaiian Fried Brown Rice (page 100), Roasted Veggie and Fig Farro Salad (page 110) and Breakfast Quinoa with Caramelized Bananas and Almond Butter (page 113).

Furthermore, this chapter will show you how to use vegetables in unique, delicious ways. For instance, you can use a sweet potato as a bun to make my California Sliders with Everything Bagel–Spiced Sweet Potato "Buns" (page 93). Or you can use vegetables as noodles, like my Pesto Veggie Noodles with Roasted Cherry Tomatoes (page 96). You can even use cauliflower in lieu of meat to make wings—the Korean Barbecue Cauliflower Wings (page 90) might just surprise you! It's amazing what you can do with veggies and whole grains with just a little creativity.

PHILLY CHEESESTEAK–STUFFED PEPPERS

These Philly cheesesteak–stuffed peppers are magic: Perfectly seasoned, saucy meat, rich and flavorful caramelized onions and mushrooms and ooey-gooey provolone cheese are all stuffed into green bell peppers and baked until the bell peppers are tender and the cheese is golden-brown delicious. It's everything you love about a Philly cheesesteak but without the starchy, carb-heavy bun! Instead, this recipe is loaded with veggies, lean meat and fiber-rich brown rice.

YIELD: 8 SERVINGS

4 large bell peppers

2 tbsp (30 ml) extra virgin olive oil, divided

1¾ tsp (9 g) salt, divided

½ tsp black pepper, divided

½ cup (38 g) diced cremini mushrooms

½ small white onion, diced

1 lb (454 g) lean ground beef

2 to 3 cloves garlic, minced

2½ tbsp (38 g) tomato paste

2 tbsp (30 ml) Worcestershire sauce

2 tsp (10 g) Dijon mustard

½ cup (120 ml) beef broth

1 cup (161 g) cooked brown rice

8 slices provolone cheese

2 tbsp (6 g) finely chopped fresh parsley

Extra Swap: I use lean ground beef instead of beef with a higher fat content in order to reduce the fat and calories of the dish.

Preheat the oven to 375°F (191°C).

Cut the tops off of the bell peppers. Use the scraps from the tops to dice ½ cup (75 g) of bell peppers. Set the diced bell peppers aside.

Remove the seeds and ribs from the bell peppers to create a hollow cavity in each bell pepper. Cut the bell peppers in half. Drizzle ½ tablespoon (8 ml) of the oil over the bell peppers, then season the bell peppers with ½ teaspoon of the salt and ¼ teaspoon of the black pepper.

Place the bell peppers, skin side down, on a medium baking sheet. Bake the bell peppers for 15 minutes.

Meanwhile, heat 1 tablespoon (15 ml) of the oil in a large skillet over medium-low heat. Add the diced bell peppers, mushrooms and onion. Cook the vegetables for about 10 minutes, until they have softened and are starting to caramelize. Add ½ teaspoon of salt and cook the vegetables for 2 minutes. Remove the cooked vegetables from the skillet.

Heat the remaining ½ tablespoon (8 ml) of oil in the skillet over medium heat. Add the beef and cook it for 5 to 7 minutes, until it's brown on the outside and slightly pink in the middle. Add the garlic and ½ teaspoon of salt and cook the mixture for about 1 minute, until the garlic is fragrant. Add the cooked vegetables to the beef and stir to combine.

Add the tomato paste, Worcestershire sauce and mustard. Stir to thoroughly combine the ingredients. Add the broth and stir until the beef and vegetables are well coated in the sauce.

Add the brown rice and stir it into the meat mixture. Season the mixture with the remaining ¼ teaspoon of salt and the remaining ¼ teaspoon of black pepper.

Divide the meat mixture among the bell pepper halves. Top each bell pepper with a slice of the provolone cheese.

Bake the bell peppers for 12 to 15 minutes, or until the cheese is golden brown and the bell peppers are tender. Top the bell pepper halves with parsley and serve.

ASIAN CHICKEN LETTUCE WRAPS

This meal was inspired by my mother-in-law, Ann. One of the first meals she cooked for me was her Asian chicken lettuce wraps, and I instantly fell in love. The dish consists of crunchy, cool lettuce cups topped with tender ground chicken that's smothered in a spicy peanut sauce and garnished with peanuts and a little Sriracha. It's a bold, satisfying and low-carb meal. I knew I had to re-create it for this cookbook and share it with all of you!

YIELD: 8 TO 10 SERVINGS

Peanut Sauce

3 tbsp (45 ml) soy sauce

2½ tbsp (40 g) peanut butter

1 tbsp (15 ml) rice wine vinegar

1½ tbsp (23 ml) honey

1 tbsp (15 ml) toasted sesame oil

2 tsp (12 g) sambal chili paste or 2 tsp (10 ml) Sriracha

2 to 3 cloves garlic, finely chopped

1 tbsp (9 g) finely chopped ginger

Lettuce Wraps

1 tbsp (15 ml) extra virgin olive oil, divided

½ cup (75 g) diced red bell pepper

⅓ cup (47 g) diced water chestnuts

4 green onions, coarsely chopped, green and white parts separated, divided

½ tsp salt, divided

1 lb (454 g) ground chicken

1 large head Bibb lettuce, sectioned into lettuce cups

¼ cup (40 g) crushed peanuts

4 to 6 lime wedges

1 to 2 tsp (5 to 10 ml) Sriracha (optional)

To make the peanut sauce, combine the soy sauce, peanut butter, vinegar, honey, sesame oil, sambal chili paste, garlic and ginger in a small microwave-safe bowl. Microwave the sauce for 30 seconds and stir it until it is smooth.

To make the lettuce wraps, heat ½ tablespoon (8 ml) of the olive oil in a large skillet or wok over medium heat. Add the bell pepper, water chestnuts, the white parts of the green onions and ¼ teaspoon of the salt. Sauté the vegetables for 4 to 6 minutes, or until they are slightly caramelized and tender. Remove the vegetables from the skillet. Return the skillet to the heat.

Add the remaining ½ tablespoon (7 ml) of olive oil and the chicken to the skillet. Cook the chicken for 3 to 5 minutes, breaking it up into small pieces as it cooks, until it is no longer pink in the middle. Season the cooked chicken with the remaining ¼ teaspoon of salt. Drain all but 1 tablespoon (15 ml) of the juices from the skillet. Return the vegetables to the skillet and stir so that they are well incorporated with the chicken.

Pour the sauce over the chicken and stir so that the sauce coats all of the meat. Taste and adjust seasonings as necessary.

Fill the lettuce cups with the desired amount of the chicken filling. Garnish the lettuce wraps with the crushed peanuts, lime wedges, Sriracha (if using) and the green parts of the green onions.

Extra Swap: I use unrefined, natural honey in place of nutrient-void white sugar.

KOREAN BARBECUE CAULIFLOWER WINGS

These wings are bursting with so much flavor and texture, you will never miss the meat. The cauliflower is cut into florets, so it mimics the look of a chicken drumstick. The florets are then coated in a rice flour batter and baked to produce crunchy, toothsome wings. The rice flour is an excellent gluten-free, healthy carb option as it is high in protein and vitamins. The rice flour also provides a light, crispy, airy texture to the wings. Finally, the wings are smothered in a sweet and spicy Korean-inspired barbecue sauce and broiled, so that the sauce is sticky and caramelized. These wings are addictively good, and it's hard to eat just one!

YIELD: 4 TO 6 SERVINGS

Korean Barbecue Sauce

½ cup (120 ml) low-sodium soy sauce

¼ cup (60 ml) water

1 tbsp (15 ml) toasted sesame oil

¼ cup (36 g) brown sugar

2 tbsp (30 ml) honey (see Note)

2 tbsp (30 ml) rice wine vinegar

1 tbsp (18 g) gochujang or Sriracha

1 tbsp (9 g) minced garlic

½ tbsp (5 g) minced ginger

1 tbsp (9 g) cornstarch

1 tbsp (15 ml) cold water

To make the Korean barbecue sauce, whisk together the soy sauce, water, oil, brown sugar, honey, vinegar, gochujang, garlic and ginger in a medium saucepan over medium-high heat. Cook the mixture for about 5 minutes, until the brown sugar is dissolved and the sauce comes to a gentle boil. Reduce the heat to medium-low and bring the sauce to a simmer.

In a small bowl, combine the cornstarch and cold water and whisk the mixture until no lumps are present. Add the cornstarch slurry to the sauce and stir until it is well incorporated.

Increase the heat to medium-high and bring the sauce back to a gentle boil. Cook the sauce for 3 to 5 minutes, until it thickens slightly; it should be able to coat the back of a spoon. Remove the sauce from the heat and allow it to cool slightly. It will thicken more as it cools.

(Continued)

Cauliflower Wings

1 cup (151 g) rice flour

1 cup (240 ml) unsweetened plain almond milk or cashew milk

½ tsp gochujang or Sriracha

1 tsp (5 g) garlic powder

¼ tsp ground ginger

1 tsp salt

1 (2½-lb [1.1-kg]) head cauliflower, cut into medium-sized florets

1 tbsp (6 g) finely chopped green onions

1 tbsp (9 g) sesame seeds

To make the cauliflower wings, preheat the oven to 425°F (218°C). Line a large baking sheet with parchment paper.

In a large bowl, combine the flour, almond milk, gochujang, garlic powder, ginger and salt and stir the ingredients until they create a thick batter. Add the cauliflower florets and stir until all of the florets are well coated in the batter.

Transfer the florets to the prepared baking sheet. Spray the florets lightly with cooking spray.

Bake the cauliflower wings for 12 minutes. Flip them and bake them for 8 to 10 minutes.

Using a grill brush or spoon, coat the wings with about ⅓ cup (80 ml) of the Korean barbecue sauce. Bake the wings for 2 to 4 minutes, or until the sauce starts to bubble.

Increase the oven's temperature to broil.

While the oven is coming to temperature, coat the wings with another ⅓ cup (80 ml) of the sauce. Broil the cauliflower wings for 1 to 3 minutes, until the sauce caramelizes—watch them carefully, so that they do not burn.

Transfer the wings to a serving dish. Garnish them with the green onions and sesame seeds.

Note: If you would prefer to make these wings vegan, you can substitute maple syrup for the honey.

Extra Swap: I use almond milk instead of full-fat dairy milk—this swap cuts the fat and calories in this dish and makes it dairy-free as well.

CALIFORNIA SLIDERS WITH EVERYTHING BAGEL—SPICED SWEET POTATO "BUNS"

There's nothing better than juicy beef sliders topped with creamy Havarti cheese, a fresh and bright guacamole and tangy pickled red onions on sweet potato "buns." Baked sweet potato rounds make a perfect low-carb bun substitute. They are simple to make and add a little sweetness to the sliders, helping round out the savory flavors. These sliders are a unique, fun, tasty way to use sweet potatoes and still enjoy a juicy, decadent burger without all the carbs!

YIELD: 6 SERVINGS

Pickled Red Onions

1 cup (130 g) thinly sliced red onions

½ cup (120 ml) red wine vinegar

¼ cup (60 ml) apple cider vinegar

½ cup (120 ml) water

1 tsp salt

3 tbsp (45 ml) agave

1 dried bay leaf

¼ tsp black peppercorns

2 to 3 whole cloves

Sliders

1½ lb (680 g) lean ground beef

2 tsp (6 g) garlic salt, divided

½ tsp black pepper

2½ tsp (13 ml) Worcestershire sauce

2 tsp (10 g) Dijon mustard

2 large Japanese sweet potatoes, cut into 12 (½" [13-mm]) rounds

1 tbsp (15 ml) extra virgin olive oil

½ tsp salt

¼ tsp black pepper

½ tbsp (5 g) everything bagel seasoning

6 slices Havarti cheese

To make the pickled red onions, place the red onions in a 16-ounce (480-ml) Mason jar or small bowl.

In a small saucepan over medium-low heat, combine the red wine vinegar, apple cider vinegar, water, salt, agave, bay leaf, peppercorns and cloves. Bring the pickling liquid to a gentle boil and cook it for 5 to 7 minutes, until the ingredients are well combined and the liquid is fragrant.

Remove the saucepan from the heat and carefully pour the hot pickling liquid over the red onions.

Allow the onions to cool completely. Once they have cooled, transfer the Mason jar to the refrigerator for at least 1 hour or up to overnight.

To make the sliders, combine the beef, 1½ teaspoons (5 g) of the garlic salt, black pepper, Worcestershire sauce and mustard in a large bowl. Mix the ingredients until they are well combined. Form the beef mixture into six slider patties. Top the patties with the remaining ½ teaspoon of garlic salt. Set the sliders aside.

Preheat the oven to 375°F (191°C).

In a large ziplock bag or bowl, combine the sweet potato rounds, oil, salt and black pepper. Seal and shake the bag or toss the sweet potatoes in the bowl with your hands until they are fully coated in the oil and seasonings. Transfer the sweet potatoes to a large baking sheet, making sure they are not touching. Sprinkle the everything bagel seasoning on six of the sweet potato rounds. These will be the top "buns."

Bake the "buns" for 15 to 20 minutes, flipping them halfway through the baking time. The "buns" should be golden brown on the outside and tender on the inside.

(Continued)

Guacamole

1 large avocado

1 tbsp (15 ml) fresh lime juice

½ tsp Worcestershire sauce

¼ tsp salt

For Serving

1 to 2 tbsp (15 to 30 g) Dijon mustard

Meanwhile, heat a grill to 400°F (204°C) or a large grill pan over medium-high heat. Cook the sliders for 3 to 4 minutes per side for medium-rare. During the last minute of cooking on the second side, place a slice of Havarti cheese on the sliders. Cook the sliders until the cheese is completely melted. Remove the sliders from the grill and allow them to rest for 5 minutes.

Meanwhile, make the guacamole. In a small bowl, mash the avocado. Add the lime juice, Worcestershire sauce and salt. Stir to thoroughly combine the ingredients.

Top an unseasoned bottom "bun" with a slider patty, some of the pickled red onions, some of the guacamole and Dijon mustard. Top the slider with a seasoned top "bun." Repeat this process until all of the sliders and buns are used.

Extra Swap: The pickled red onions are refined sugar-free and sweetened only with agave.

PESTO VEGGIE NOODLES WITH ROASTED CHERRY TOMATOES

Veggie noodles are a great low-carb alternative to refined pastas. Using a spiralizer, you can create long, curly strands of vegetables that resemble noodles. For this dish, I paired sweet potato noodles with zucchini noodles for extra color and nutrients. The noodles are lightly sautéed and dressed with a bright, herbaceous pesto. Finally, I topped the noodles with roasted cherry tomatoes for a pop of juicy, sweet goodness.

YIELD: 4 SERVINGS

Roasted Cherry Tomatoes

1¼ cups (186 g) cherry tomatoes

1 tbsp (15 ml) extra virgin olive oil

1 tbsp (15 ml) balsamic vinegar

¼ tsp salt

Pinch of black pepper

Pesto

2 to 3 cloves garlic

¼ cup (34 g) pine nuts

1 tbsp (6 g) lemon zest

1½ cups (24 g) fresh basil leaves

½ tsp salt

Pinch of black pepper

3 tbsp (45 ml) fresh lemon juice

⅓ cup (80 ml) extra virgin olive oil

¼ cup (45 g) grated Parmesan cheese

Veggie Noodles

2 cups (226 g) zucchini noodles (see Note)

½ tsp salt, divided

1 to 2 tbsp (15 to 30 ml) extra virgin olive oil, divided

4 cups (452 g) sweet potato noodles or butternut squash noodles (see Note)

For Serving

¼ cup (34 g) toasted pine nuts or toasted walnuts

¼ cup (28 g) shaved fresh Parmesan cheese

To make the roasted cherry tomatoes, preheat the oven to 400°F (204°C). Place the cherry tomatoes on a medium baking sheet. Drizzle the cherry tomatoes with the oil and vinegar, then season them with the salt and black pepper. Roast the tomatoes for 12 to 15 minutes, stirring them halfway through the cooking time, or until they are juicy and beginning to burst.

While the tomatoes are roasting, make the pesto. Combine the garlic, pine nuts and lemon zest in a small food processor. Process until the pine nuts are broken down and the mixture has a sand-like consistency. Add the basil, salt, black pepper and lemon juice. Process until the basil is well incorporated into the mixture. With the processor running, slowly drizzle in the oil and continue processing the pesto until it is homogenous and velvety. Gently mix in the grated Parmesan cheese. Set the pesto aside.

To prepare the veggie noodles, place the zucchini noodles on a layer of paper towels. Sprinkle a dash of the salt on the zucchini noodles to draw out any excess moisture and let them sit undisturbed for 5 to 10 minutes. Gather up the paper towels with the zucchini inside and wring the paper towels to squeeze out as much of the excess water from the zucchini as possible.

Heat 1 tablespoon (15 ml) of the oil in a large skillet over medium heat. Add the sweet potato noodles and ¼ teaspoon of the salt and sauté the sweet potato noodles for 6 to 8 minutes, or until they are slightly browned but still crunchy. Add the zucchini noodles, the remaining 1 tablespoon (15 ml) of oil if the skillet is dry and the remaining ¼ teaspoon of salt. Cook the noodles for 1 to 2 minutes, until the zucchini noodles are heated through.

Remove the noodles from the heat and add the desired amount of the pesto. Toss the noodles to coat them with the pesto. Divide the noodles among four bowls. Top each serving with the roasted cherry tomatoes, toasted pine nuts and shaved Parmesan cheese.

Note: If you're wondering how many sweet potatoes and zucchini to buy for this recipe, generally 2 medium sweet potatoes or one medium butternut squash will yield 4 cups (452 g) of noodles and 2 medium zucchini will yield 2 cups (226 g) of noodles.

MEDITERRANEAN MINI CRUSTLESS QUICHES

These Mediterranean mini crustless quiches are a delicious, easy, low-carb breakfast treat! You can make them in fewer than 30 minutes, and there's no pesky crust involved. The individual-sized quiches are bursting with delicious, vibrant Mediterranean flavors like pancetta, sun-dried tomatoes, spinach and feta. Plus, they are made healthier by substituting heavy cream with Greek yogurt, which makes them light, fluffy and protein rich. This is a grab-and-go powerhouse breakfast perfect for busy mornings.

YIELD: 10 SERVINGS

¼ cup (60 ml) unsweetened plain almond milk or cashew milk

¼ cup (71 g) plain Greek yogurt

8 large eggs

¾ tsp salt, divided

½ tsp black pepper

½ cup (56 g) diced pancetta or bacon

½ tbsp (8 ml) extra virgin olive oil

1 (5-oz [142-g]) bag baby spinach

½ cup (55 g) sun-dried tomatoes packed in oil, rinsed

2 to 3 cloves garlic, finely chopped

1 tbsp (15 ml) fresh lemon juice

⅓ cup (50 g) crumbled feta cheese

Preheat the oven to 350°F (177°C). Grease ten cavities of a twelve-cavity muffin pan.

In a large bowl, whisk together the almond milk and Greek yogurt. Add the eggs, ½ teaspoon of the salt and black pepper. Whisk the ingredients until they are well combined.

In a large skillet over medium heat, cook the pancetta for 5 to 8 minutes, until the fat is rendered and the pancetta is crispy. Remove the pancetta from the skillet and remove all but ½ tablespoon (8 ml) of the excess fat. Return the skillet to medium heat.

Add the oil to the skillet. Add the spinach and the remaining ¼ teaspoon of salt and cook the spinach for 4 to 6 minutes, until it is wilted. Add the sun-dried tomatoes and garlic and cook the mixture for 2 to 3 minutes, until the garlic is fragrant. Add the pancetta and stir to combine the ingredients. Stir in the lemon juice.

Divide the egg mixture between the prepared muffin cavities. Divide the spinach mixture between the egg cups and use a spoon to gently mix the eggs and spinach mixture. Top each egg cup with the feta cheese.

Bake the quiches for 12 to 15 minutes, or until they are golden brown on top and no longer jiggly in the middle; they will have risen slightly, like a soufflé, but they will sink back down as they cool.

Serve the quiches while they are warm.

Note: These crustless quiches are great for meal prep, because they store well in the refrigerator up to 1 week. When you are ready to eat, microwave them for 1 to 2 minutes, or until they are heated all the way through.

HAWAIIAN FRIED BROWN RICE

This is a healthier, Hawaiian twist on a classic Chinese takeout favorite. I replace the white rice with fiber-rich brown rice. The brown rice is fried with eggs and peas, just like the traditional takeout version, and it's tossed in a citrusy umami-packed sauce. Ham and pineapple bring the Hawaiian vibes to the party. Finally, the dish is topped with Sriracha for spice, cilantro for freshness and cashews for crunch. It's a super quick and healthy meal that's perfect for busy weeknights.

YIELD: 4 TO 6 SERVINGS

Sauce

2 tbsp (30 ml) ponzu sauce

2 tbsp (30 ml) soy sauce

2 tbsp (30 ml) sweet chili sauce (such as Sky Valley brand)

1 tbsp (15 ml) toasted sesame oil

1 to 2 tsp (5 to 10 ml) Sriracha

Rice

1½ to 2 tbsp (23 to 30 g) coconut oil, divided

⅓ cup + 2 tbsp (50 g) coarsely chopped roasted unsalted cashews, divided

¾ cup (101 g) cubed thick-cut ham or chicken andouille sausage

½ small red onion, diced

½ tsp salt

½ cup (83 g) diced fresh pineapple

½ cup (67 g) fresh or frozen peas

2 to 3 cloves garlic, finely chopped

2 tsp (6 g) minced ginger

2 large eggs, beaten

3 cups (585 g) cooked brown rice (see Note)

Sriracha, as needed

2 tbsp (6 g) finely chopped fresh cilantro

To make the sauce, whisk together the ponzu sauce, soy sauce, sweet chili sauce, sesame oil and Sriracha in a small bowl. Set the sauce aside.

To make the rice, heat ½ tablespoon (7 g) of the coconut oil in a large skillet over medium heat. Add the cashews and cook them for 2 to 3 minutes, until they are golden brown. Remove the cashews from the skillet.

Heat ½ tablespoon (7 g) of the coconut oil in the skillet over medium heat. Add the ham and cook it for 3 to 5 minutes, until it forms a golden-brown crust and is warmed through. Remove the ham from the skillet.

Heat ½ tablespoon (7 g) of coconut oil. Add the onion and cook it for 2 to 3 minutes, or until it has softened. Add the salt, pineapple and peas and cook the mixture for 1 to 2 minutes. Add the garlic and ginger and cook the mixture for 1 to 2 minutes, or until the garlic is fragrant.

Push the vegetable mixture to the side of the skillet. If the skillet is dry, add the remaining ½ tablespoon (7 g) of coconut oil and allow it to melt. Add the eggs and continually stir them for 2 to 3 minutes, until small curds are created and the eggs are fully cooked. Add the rice and mix it with the eggs and vegetables. Add ⅓ cup (43 g) of the cashews. Pour in the sauce and toss the fried rice to coat everything in the sauce.

Divide the fried rice among four to six bowls. Top each serving with the Sriracha, remaining 2 tablespoons (7 g) of the cashews and cilantro.

Note: This recipe works best if the cooked rice is a day old.

CAULIFLOWER RICE CAJUN JAMBALAYA

Cauliflower is such a versatile vegetable! You can use it in so many unique ways, including as a type of "rice." This Cauliflower Rice Cajun Jambalaya is a flavor-packed, easy and low-carb dinner option that will take you right to New Orleans. Simply grate the cauliflower until it resembles rice and then toast it with a little olive oil in the oven until it's tender and slightly crispy. Then pair the cauliflower rice with a robust jambalaya that's filled with tons of Cajun spices, three kinds of juicy proteins and a rich but light tomato-based sauce. It's a fun, unique and healthy weeknight meal!

YIELD: 6 TO 8 SERVINGS

Cajun Spice Blend

1 tbsp (9 g) smoked paprika

½ tbsp (5 g) onion powder

½ tbsp (5 g) garlic powder

½ tsp dried oregano

½ tsp dried thyme

½ tsp paprika

2 tsp (10 g) salt

¼ tsp cayenne pepper

¼ tsp black pepper

½ tsp white pepper

Jambalaya

4 tbsp (60 ml) extra virgin olive oil, divided

4 cups (452 g) fresh cauliflower rice

1 tsp salt, divided

2 large boneless, skinless chicken breasts, cut into small pieces

Pinch of black pepper

4 precooked chicken andouille sausages, thickly sliced

1 lb (454 g) fresh shrimp, peeled and deveined

1 small onion, diced

2 large carrots, diced

2 large ribs celery, diced

3 to 4 cloves garlic, minced

To make the Cajun spice blend, whisk together the smoked paprika, onion powder, garlic powder, oregano, thyme, paprika, salt, cayenne pepper, black pepper and white pepper in a small bowl. Set the bowl aside.

To make the jambalaya, preheat the oven to 400°F (204°C). Lightly grease a large baking sheet.

Drizzle 1 tablespoon (15 ml) of the oil over the cauliflower rice, then sprinkle it with ½ teaspoon of the salt. Roast the cauliflower for 15 to 20 minutes, stirring it halfway through the cooking time, until the cauliflower rice is tender and starting to brown.

Meanwhile, heat 1 tablespoon (15 ml) of the oil in a large cast-iron skillet or Dutch oven over medium heat. Cook the chicken for 5 to 8 minutes, until its internal temperature reaches 165°F (74°C). Remove the chicken from the skillet. Season the chicken with ¼ teaspoon of the salt and the black pepper.

Heat ½ tablespoon (8 ml) of the oil in the skillet. Add the sausage and cook it for 4 to 5 minutes, until each side is browned. Remove the sausage from the skillet.

Heat 1 tablespoon (15 ml) of the oil in the skillet. Add the shrimp and cook them for 3 to 4 minutes, until they are opaque and light pink. Remove the shrimp from the skillet and season them with ¼ teaspoon of the salt.

Heat the remaining ½ tablespoon (7 ml) of the oil in the skillet. Add the onion, carrots and celery. Cook the vegetables for 5 to 6 minutes, until they have softened. Add the garlic and cook the mixture for 1 to 2 minutes, until the garlic is fragrant.

(Continued)

¼ cup (60 g) tomato paste

1 (28-oz [794-g]) can crushed tomatoes

1 cup (240 ml) chicken broth

1 tsp Worcestershire sauce

1 to 2 tsp (5 to 10 ml) hot sauce (such as Frank's RedHot brand), or to taste

2 dried bay leaves

Add the tomato paste and spice blend and cook the mixture for 1 to 2 minutes, until the spices are fragrant and the tomato paste is a rusty red color.

Add the crushed tomatoes, broth, Worcestershire sauce, hot sauce and bay leaves, and stir to combine the ingredients. Lower the heat and simmer the sauce for 25 to 30 minutes, so that the flavor develops and the sauce thickens slightly.

Add the chicken, sausage and shrimp during the last 4 minutes of cooking, so that they can warm through. Serve the jambalaya sauce over the cauliflower rice.

Extra Swap: I use chicken andouille sausage instead of regular andouille sausage because it contains much less fat and calories but is still just as tasty.

STEAK FAJITA BROWN RICE BOWLS

This bowl is bursting with all of your favorite fajita flavors. Juicy marinated and grilled flank steak, charred veggies, a creamy, perfectly seasoned guacamole and all of the traditional fixings make for a delicious and healthy meal. Bowls—with their colorful veggies, a healthy grain and a protein—have become very popular. And for good reason! Bowls allow you to ditch the high-carb, low-nutrient starch option for a healthy whole grain without sacrificing any flavor. The brown rice found in these bowls is a great whole-grain option, as it's gluten free, high in fiber and rich in nutrients.

YIELD: 4 TO 6 SERVINGS

Steak

½ cup (8 g) fresh cilantro

⅓ cup (80 ml) extra virgin olive oil

1 tsp chili powder

1 tsp salt

½ tsp onion powder

½ tsp ground cumin

¼ tsp black pepper

3 tbsp (45 ml) fresh lime juice

1 tbsp (6 g) lime zest

1 tbsp (9 g) diced pickled jalapeños

½ tbsp (8 ml) pickled jalapeño brine

¼ tsp agave or honey

1 tsp Worcestershire sauce

3 to 4 cloves garlic, minced

1½ lb (680 g) flank steak

Vegetables

2 tbsp (30 ml) extra virgin olive oil

½ tsp dried oregano

½ tsp salt

¼ tsp garlic powder

¼ tsp ground cumin

¼ tsp chili powder

1 small red bell pepper, thinly sliced

1 small orange bell pepper, thinly sliced

1 small yellow bell pepper, thinly sliced

1 small red onion, thinly sliced

To make the steak, combine the cilantro, oil, chili powder, salt, onion powder, cumin, black pepper, lime juice and zest, jalapeños, jalapeño brine, agave, Worcestershire and garlic in a food processor. Process the ingredients until a slightly chunky marinade forms. Place the steak in a large sealable container or ziplock bag and pour the marinade over it, making sure the whole steak is covered. Place the marinated steak in the refrigerator for at least 4 hours or up to overnight. Take the steak out of the fridge at least 30 minutes prior to grilling it.

One to two hours prior to grilling, prep the vegetables. In a small bowl, combine the oil, oregano, salt, garlic, cumin and chili powder. Place the red bell pepper, orange bell pepper, yellow bell pepper and onion in a large sealable container or ziplock bag. Pour the oil mixture over the vegetables. Seal the container or bag and allow the vegetables to marinate for 30 to 60 minutes at room temperature.

(Continued)

Guacamole

2 large avocados

Juice of ½ medium lime

½ tsp Worcestershire sauce

½ tsp garlic powder

¾ tsp salt

¼ tsp cumin

¼ tsp onion powder

¼ tsp chili powder

Pinch of black pepper

Bowls

2 cups (390 g) cooked brown rice

½ cup (143 g) plain Greek yogurt

½ cup (60 g) shredded Cheddar cheese or ½ cup (75 g) crumbled cotija cheese

2 tbsp (6 g) coarsely chopped fresh cilantro

2 tbsp (14 g) thinly sliced pickled jalapeños

Lime wedges, for garnish

To make the guacamole, combine the avocados, lime juice, Worcestershire sauce, garlic powder, salt, cumin, onion powder, chili powder and black pepper in a medium bowl. Mash the avocados until they are creamy but still a little chunky and the other ingredients are well incorporated.

Grease a large cast-iron skillet or grill roasting pan and set it over medium heat on the grill. Add the vegetables to the skillet. Cook the vegetables for 5 to 6 minutes, tossing them occasionally, until they are tender and slightly charred. Remove the vegetables and skillet or roasting pan from the grill.

Increase the grill's heat to medium-high. Add the steak directly to the grill. Cook it for 4 to 5 minutes per side, or until each side develops grill marks. Reduce the grill's temperature to low and cook the steak for 1 to 2 minutes per side, until the steak's internal temperature reaches 135°F (57°C) for medium-rare or 145°F (63°C) for medium. Allow the steak to rest for 10 minutes. Cut the steak into thin strips against the grain.

To make the bowls, place the rice in the bottom of each bowl. Top the rice with the desired amount of vegetables and steak. Place the Greek yogurt, Cheddar cheese, guacamole, cilantro and pickled jalapeños over the vegetables and steak. Garnish with the lime wedges.

Extra Swap: I use Greek yogurt in lieu of sour cream. Plain nonfat Greek yogurt tastes just like sour cream, but it contains less fat, fewer calories and more protein.

ROASTED GARLIC AND CREAM CHEESE MASHED CAULIFLOWER

Cauliflower can be mashed into creamy lusciousness just like white potatoes. Adding roasted garlic to the mash adds a robust, nutty and slightly sweet garlic flavor. The addition of cream cheese makes the mash extra creamy and rich and just a little tangy. Using cauliflower in lieu of potatoes is a great swap that allows you to still enjoy this classic side dish without all the starch.

YIELD: 6 SERVINGS

1 medium head garlic

1½ tbsp (23 ml) extra virgin olive oil, divided

Pinch of salt

1 large head cauliflower, cut into medium-sized florets

¼ cup (60 ml) plus 2 tbsp (30 ml) unsweetened plain almond milk or cashew milk, divided

2½ tbsp (38 g) whipped cream cheese

1 tbsp (15 g) butter

½ tsp garlic salt

¼ tsp lemon-pepper seasoning

Preheat the oven to 350°F (177°C). Cut off the top of the head of garlic. Place the garlic on a square piece of foil and drizzle the garlic with ½ tablespoon (8 ml) of the oil and sprinkle it with the salt. Wrap the foil around the garlic and roast it for 40 to 45 minutes, until it is very soft. Allow the garlic to cool completely. You should be able to easily squeeze the cloves of garlic out of their skins.

Bring a large pot of salted water to a boil over high heat. Boil the cauliflower for 8 to 10 minutes, or until it is fork-tender. Drain the water from the pot and transfer the cauliflower to a large food processor. Add the garlic, ¼ cup (60 ml) of the almond milk, cream cheese, butter, the remaining 1 tablespoon (15 ml) of oil, garlic salt and lemon-pepper seasoning. Process the ingredients until the cauliflower is smooth and creamy. If the mash is too thick, add the remaining 2 tablespoons (30 ml) of almond milk, 1 tablespoon (15 ml) at a time, until you reach your desired consistency.

ROASTED VEGGIE AND FIG FARRO SALAD

This salad is fall on a plate. Delicious roasted and colorful parsnips, beets and butternut squash are served with whole-grain farro, creamy and tangy goat cheese, crunchy and salty almonds, sweet and earthy dried figs and peppery arugula that are all dressed with a tangy, rich maple-balsamic dressing. Yum! Farro is a balanced, nutritious whole grain that is a healthy carb and great to incorporate into your diet because it's high in fiber, easy on digestion and rich in other nutrients like protein, fat, magnesium, vitamins and zinc. Boasting a chewy texture and roasted nutty flavor, farro makes this salad a delicious, filling lunch or dinner.

YIELD: 4 TO 6 SERVINGS

Maple-Balsamic Vinaigrette

¼ cup (60 ml) balsamic vinegar (see Note)

2 tsp (10 g) Dijon mustard

1 tbsp (15 ml) pure maple syrup

½ tsp salt

¼ tsp garlic powder

¼ cup (60 ml) extra virgin olive oil

Salad

¾ cup (180 g) uncooked farro

1 small butternut squash, peeled and cubed

1 large beet, peeled and cubed

1 large parsnip, peeled and cubed

1 small red onion, coarsely chopped

1½ tbsp (23 ml) extra virgin olive oil

1 tsp salt

½ tsp black pepper

2½ cups (50 g) fresh arugula

⅓ cup (50 g) crumbled goat cheese

⅓ cup (57 g) roasted salted almonds

⅓ cup (50 g) halved dried figs

1 tbsp (3 g) finely chopped fresh parsley

To make the maple-balsamic vinaigrette, whisk together the vinegar, mustard, maple syrup, salt and garlic powder in a small bowl. Slowly drizzle in the oil, whisking constantly, until the dressing is emulsified. Set the vinaigrette aside.

To make the salad, cook the farro according to the package's instructions. Set the farro aside.

Preheat the oven to 375°F (191°C). Lightly grease a large baking sheet.

In a large bowl, combine the butternut squash, beet, parsnip, onion, oil, salt and black pepper. Add the vegetables to the prepared baking sheet. Roast the vegetables for 25 to 30 minutes, flipping them halfway through the roasting time, until they are tender on the inside and slightly browned on the outside.

Arrange the arugula on a large serving platter or on four to six individual plates. Top the arugula with the farro, roasted vegetables, goat cheese, almonds, figs and parsley. Drizzle the salad with the desired amount of the vinaigrette.

Note: To elevate the vinaigrette even more, use a quality fig-flavored balsamic vinegar.

BREAKFAST QUINOA WITH CARAMELIZED BANANAS AND ALMOND BUTTER

Quinoa is a great substitute for many types of rice and pasta because it boasts so many great health benefits: It's naturally gluten-free, extremely high in fiber and helps control blood sugar. Its fluffy texture and mild nutty taste make it perfect for savory and sweet applications. I love to serve it for breakfast and flavor it with cinnamon, a little brown sugar and maple syrup. I also top it with caramelized bananas and creamy almond butter for a delicious, nutrient-packed breakfast.

YIELD: 4 SERVINGS

1 cup (170 g) quinoa

1¾ cups (420 ml) unsweetened plain almond milk or cashew milk, divided

⅛ tsp plus pinch of salt, divided

1 (3" [7.5-cm]) cinnamon stick

2 tbsp (18 g) brown sugar

¼ tsp ground cinnamon

2 tbsp (30 ml) pure maple syrup

1 tbsp (15 g) coconut oil

2 medium bananas, sliced into 1" (3-cm) rounds

½ cup (74 g) fresh blueberries

2 tbsp (22 g) almond butter

1 tbsp (7 g) chopped pecans

In a medium pot over high heat, combine the quinoa, 1½ cups (360 ml) of the almond milk, ⅛ teaspoon of the salt and the cinnamon stick. Bring the mixture to a boil, then reduce the heat to medium-low and bring the quinoa to a simmer. Cook the quinoa for 10 to 15 minutes, or until the almond milk is absorbed and the quinoa is fluffy. Remove the cinnamon stick.

Add the brown sugar, ground cinnamon and maple syrup. Stir to combine the ingredients, then stir in the remaining ¼ cup (60 ml) of the almond milk. Set the quinoa aside.

In a medium skillet over medium heat, melt the oil. Add the bananas and cook them for 2 to 3 minutes per side, or until each side is golden brown and caramelized. Remove the bananas from the skillet and sprinkle them with the remaining pinch of salt.

Divide the quinoa among four bowls. Top each serving with the caramelized bananas, blueberries, almond butter and pecans.

LIGHTER DAIRY DISHES *and* DESSERTS

The Swap: Lighter dairy options and dairy-free alternatives instead of heavy, caloric dairy products.

....

Confession: I'm a dairy lover. Ice cream is hands down my favorite dessert and an epic cheese plate is my go-to appetizer. I've actually been to a cheese castle in Wisconsin, and it's one of the most magical places I've visited. So I am not here to tell you to give up dairy completely. In fact, there are plenty of dairy products that are good for you and part of a balanced diet, such as Greek yogurt, cottage cheese and kefir. But I am also here to help you find ways to make every meal healthier, and minimizing heavy dairy products such as heavy cream and whole milk can make meals lighter and less caloric. You can also find the health benefits of dairy in other more nutritious ingredients, such as calcium in almonds, kale and spinach or protein in nuts and eggs.

In this chapter, you will find innovative ways to cut out heavy dairy products in the foods you love. For example, take the Creamy Cashew Alfredo (page 120) or the Thai Sweet Potato and Carrot Soup with Spiced Cashews (page 123). There's even ice cream included in this chapter—check out my Strawberry-Banana Nice Cream on page 127.

You don't need dairy to make creamy, dreamy foods, and this chapter will show you how to cook confidently with less dairy!

HEALTHY SMOKED GOUDA AND CHEDDAR MAC AND CHEESE

Mac and cheese is a classic, nostalgic comfort food. The only problem is that mac and cheese can result in a carb and dairy overload. So in this recipe, I replace some of the heavy dairy to lighten up a beloved dish. I use ghee and almond milk in place of regular butter and full-fat dairy milk. This dish is not completely dairy-free because I do use real cheese—it is mac and cheese, after all! But I use only all-natural, real cheese, and I even include some broccoli to keep this mac and cheese light and healthy.

YIELD: 6 TO 8 SERVINGS

1 small head broccoli, cut into small florets

1 tbsp (15 ml) extra virgin olive oil

1 tsp salt, divided

¼ tsp black pepper

10 oz (284 g) whole-wheat cavatappi or rotini

3 tbsp (44 g) ghee, divided

2½ tbsp (20 g) whole-wheat flour

1½ cups (360 ml) unsweetened plain almond milk or cashew milk, at room temperature

½ tsp mustard powder

1 tsp garlic powder

⅛ tsp ground nutmeg

Heaping ½ cup (60 g) shredded smoked Gouda cheese

Heaping ½ cup (60 g) shredded sharp Cheddar cheese

Heaping ½ cup (60 g) cream Havarti cheese

⅔ cup (60 g) whole-wheat panko breadcrumbs

1 tsp garlic salt

½ tsp Italian seasoning

Preheat the oven to 400°F (204°C).

On a large baking sheet, toss the broccoli with the oil, ½ teaspoon of the salt and black pepper. Roast the broccoli for 15 to 20 minutes, flipping the broccoli halfway through the roasting time, until the broccoli is browned.

Bring a large pot of salted water to a boil over high heat. Boil the cavatappi pasta to al dente, according to the package's instructions. Drain the pasta, reserving ½ cup (120 ml) of the cooking water.

While the pasta is cooking, heat a large saucepan over medium heat. Add 2 tablespoons (30 g) of the ghee. When the ghee has melted, add the flour. Using a spatula, mix the ingredients for 3 to 5 minutes, until the flour absorbs all of the ghee and a paste-like mixture forms.

Whisking constantly, slowly add the almond milk, a little at a time. Add the mustard powder, garlic powder and nutmeg. Bring the mixture to a gentle simmer and cook it for 5 to 6 minutes, whisking constantly, until it has thickened slightly.

Add the Gouda cheese, whisking until it has melted into the sauce. Add the Cheddar cheese, whisking until it has melted into the sauce. Add the cream Havarti cheese, whisking until it has melted into the sauce. Remove the sauce from the heat. Season the sauce with the remaining ½ teaspoon of salt.

Add the pasta to the sauce, tossing to coat the pasta with the sauce. Add some of the pasta cooking water to thin the sauce, if needed. Add the broccoli to the mac and cheese. Taste the mac and cheese and add additional salt if needed.

To make the whole-wheat breadcrumbs, melt the remaining 1 tablespoon (14 g) of ghee in a medium skillet. Add the breadcrumbs and cook until slightly toasted, 5 to 6 minutes. Add in the garlic salt and the Italian seasoning and stir until well-combined. Top the mac and cheese with toasted breadcrumbs.

Extra Swap: I use a whole-grain pasta instead of white, starchy pasta.

CHOPPED ITALIAN SALAD WITH CRISPY GARLIC CHICKPEAS

This bright and colorful dish proves that you don't need a creamy, mayo-based or dairy-filled dressing to achieve a delicious, crowd-pleasing salad. This salad uses a bright, lemony and herby dressing that gives the salad tons of flavor without heavy dairy products. The salad also has all of the classic fixings of a great Italian chopped salad and is topped with crispy, garlicky roasted chickpeas for an additional pop of crunch and flavor.

YIELD: 8 TO 10 SERVINGS

Crispy Garlic Chickpeas

1 (15-oz [425-g]) can chickpeas, drained, rinsed and dried

½ tbsp (8 ml) extra virgin olive oil

½ tsp salt

½ tsp garlic powder

Dressing

2 tbsp (30 ml) fresh lemon juice

1 tbsp (15 g) plus 1 tsp Dijon mustard

2 tbsp (30 ml) red wine vinegar

2 tsp (10 ml) honey

1 tsp Italian seasoning

2 to 3 cloves garlic, minced

¼ cup (60 ml) extra virgin olive oil

Salt, as needed

Black pepper, as needed

Chopped Italian Salad

1 large head romaine lettuce, coarsely chopped

1 cup (175 g) halved cherry tomatoes

½ small red onion, thinly sliced

½ cup (69 g) coarsely chopped turkey pepperoni

5 oz (142 g) fresh mozzarella pearls

⅓ cup (80 g) thinly sliced pickled banana peppers

¼ cup (32 g) pre-sliced black olives

4 to 5 large leaves fresh basil, coarsely chopped

To make the crispy garlic chickpeas, preheat the oven to 400°F (204°C).

In a medium bowl, combine the chickpeas, oil, salt and garlic powder. Shake the bowl until all of the chickpeas are evenly coated in the oil mixture. Spread out the chickpeas on a medium baking sheet.

Bake the chickpeas for 22 to 28 minutes, stirring them occasionally, until they are golden brown and crispy.

To make the dressing, combine the lemon juice, mustard, vinegar, honey, Italian seasoning, garlic, oil, salt and black pepper in a small salad shaker or lidded jar. Seal the container and shake it vigorously until the dressing is emulsified.

To make the chopped Italian salad, combine the lettuce, cherry tomatoes, onion, pepperoni, mozzarella pearls, banana peppers, olives and basil in a large bowl. Top the salad with the dressing and toss the salad until all of the ingredients are mixed and coated in the dressing. Top the salad with the crispy garlic chickpeas.

Extra Swap: I use turkey pepperoni instead of regular pepperoni, because turkey pepperoni is not as greasy and fatty.

CREAMY CASHEW ALFREDO

This cashew alfredo sauce is so creamy and luscious, you would never guess it's made without heavy cream or butter. Cashews are a magical ingredient that, when blended with liquid, transform into a velvety cream. Then it's just a matter of adding flavor: roasted onion and garlic for depth of flavor, almond milk and vegetable broth for richness and extra creaminess and grated Parmesan—or nutritional yeast to make the dish completely dairy-free—for umami. Toss this sauce with gluten-free fettuccine noodles to create a delicious, easy and nutrient-rich meal.

YIELD: 6 TO 8 SERVINGS

1½ cups (180 g) raw cashews

12 oz (340 g) gluten-free fettuccine or pasta of choice

1 tbsp (15 ml) extra virgin olive oil

½ medium sweet onion, diced

3 to 4 cloves garlic, minced

1½ tsp (8 g) salt, divided

¾ cup (180 ml) unsweetened plain almond milk or cashew milk

¾ cup (180 ml) vegetable broth, plus more as needed

2 tbsp (30 ml) fresh lemon juice

½ tsp onion powder

½ tsp garlic powder

½ tsp black pepper

¼ cup (45 g) grated Parmesan cheese or nutritional yeast

2 tbsp (6 g) finely chopped fresh parsley

Soak the cashews in room-temperature water overnight or in boiling water for 5 to 10 minutes. This helps soften the cashews, so that they blend easily into the sauce. Drain and rinse the cashews.

In a pot of heavily salted water, cook the fettuccine according to the package's instructions. Reserve ¼ cup (60 ml) of the pasta cooking water in a small bowl or measuring cup. Return the cooked pasta to the pot.

Heat the oil in a medium skillet over medium heat. Add the onion and cook it for 3 to 5 minutes, until it is tender and translucent. Add the garlic and ½ teaspoon of the salt and cook the mixture for 2 to 3 minutes, or until the garlic is fragrant.

Transfer the cashews and onion mixture to a food processor or high-power blender. Add the almond milk, broth, lemon juice, onion powder, garlic powder, black pepper and remaining 1 teaspoon of salt. Process the ingredients until they are smooth—it may take several minutes for the cashews to break down and form a creamy, smooth sauce. If the sauce is too thick and grainy, add a little more broth and continue to process until the sauce is smooth. Add the Parmesan cheese and mix until it is well incorporated into the sauce.

Top the pasta with the desired amount of sauce. Toss the pasta so that all of the noodles are coated in the sauce, adding a little of the reserved pasta cooking water to thin the sauce if necessary.

Top the pasta with the parsley and serve.

Note: This meal would be great served with grilled chicken or another lean protein.

Extra Swap: I pair the sauce with protein- and fiber-packed gluten-free chickpea noodles (such as Banza brand) instead of starchy white-flour noodles.

THAI SWEET POTATO AND CARROT SOUP WITH SPICED CASHEWS

This Thai sweet potato soup, with its velvety texture and spicy kick, is like a big, warm, comforting hug! It's hard to believe there is no milk or heavy cream in this recipe—the creaminess is achieved with coconut milk and softened sweet potatoes and carrots. Plus, the coconut milk, miso, curry paste and spices give this soup tons of flavor, making it addictively good. It just so happens to be vegan, gluten free and dairy free too.

YIELD: 8 SERVINGS

Spiced Cashews

2 tsp (10 ml) melted coconut oil

1 tsp soy sauce

¼ tsp curry powder

¼ tsp ground turmeric

¼ tsp garlic powder

⅛ tsp cayenne pepper

½ tsp brown sugar

½ tsp salt

¾ cup (90 g) raw cashews

Thai Sweet Potato and Carrot Soup

1 tbsp (15 ml) extra virgin olive oil

1 small white onion, diced

3 to 4 cloves garlic, minced

1 tbsp (9 g) grated ginger

2 large sweet potatoes, peeled and diced

5 medium carrots, peeled and diced

1½ to 2 tbsp (23 to 31 g) red curry paste

1½ tsp (9 g) white miso paste

2 cups (480 ml) vegetable broth, plus more as needed

1 (15-oz [444-ml]) can light or full-fat coconut milk

2 tbsp (30 ml) soy sauce

½ to ¾ tsp salt (optional)

¼ tsp black pepper (optional)

1 to 2 tbsp (3 to 6 g) coarsely chopped fresh cilantro

8 lime wedges

To make the spiced cashews, preheat the oven to 375°F (191°C). Line a medium baking sheet with parchment paper.

In a small bowl, combine the coconut oil, soy sauce, curry powder, turmeric, garlic powder, cayenne pepper, brown sugar and salt. Add the cashews and stir until all of the cashews are fully coated in the oil mixture. Transfer the nuts to the prepared baking sheet. Roast the cashews for 5 to 6 minutes, flipping them halfway through the roasting time, or until they are golden brown. Set the cashews aside.

To make the Thai sweet potato and carrot soup, heat the olive oil in a large pot over medium heat. Add the onion and cook it for 1 to 2 minutes, or until it is translucent. Add the garlic and ginger and cook the mixture for 1 minute, until the garlic and ginger are fragrant.

Increase the heat to medium-high. Add the sweet potatoes and carrots. Sauté them for about 5 minutes, until they are slightly soft.

Stir in the curry paste and miso paste, and cook the mixture for 1 to 2 minutes, until the pastes are fragrant. Add the broth, coconut milk and soy sauce, stirring to combine the ingredients. Bring the soup to a boil, reduce the heat to medium-low and simmer the soup for 20 to 25 minutes, until the sweet potatoes are tender.

Using an immersion blender, blend the soup until it is smooth and creamy, adding more broth if desired to adjust the thickness of the soup. Alternatively, carefully transfer the soup to a countertop blender and blend the soup until it is creamy. Taste the soup and season it with the salt (if using) and black pepper (if using).

Ladle the soup into eight bowls. Top each serving with the spiced cashews, cilantro and 1 lime wedge.

Extra Swap: I garnish the soup with spiced cashews, which are gluten free and packed with protein, in lieu of starchy croutons.

GARLIC-LEMON HUMMUS

My mom and I love to throw parties, and we often complain that it's hard to make a delicious appetizer without cream cheese, heavy cream or shredded cheese. But this hummus is about to prove that theory wrong. Hummus stars chickpeas and tahini, which are packed with plant-based protein, essential minerals and fiber. Blended with a few other simple ingredients, it creates a smooth, velvety dip. This Garlic-Lemon Hummus is as creamy and flavorful as any cheese and dairy-filled appetizer. It has a luscious, smooth texture and is packed with big lemon and garlic flavor and served with warm, toasted whole-wheat naan. It's the delicious and nutritious treat to wow your guest at a party—or to just eat during the week!

YIELD: 10 TO 12 SERVINGS

2 (15-oz [425-g]) cans chickpeas, rinsed and drained

½ tsp baking soda

¾ cup (168 g) tahini

4 to 5 cloves garlic

5 tbsp (75 ml) fresh lemon juice

1 tbsp (6 g) lemon zest

¾ tsp ground cumin

1¼ tsp (6 g) salt, divided

5 tbsp (75 ml) extra virgin olive oil, divided, plus more for garnish

2 to 4 tbsp (30 to 60 ml) ice water

2 whole-wheat naan flatbreads

1 tsp za'atar or everything bagel seasoning, plus more for garnish

2 large carrots, peeled and cut into sticks.

3 medium radishes, sliced

1 medium cucumber, sliced

Preheat the oven to 375°F (191°C).

In a medium pot over medium-high heat, combine the chickpeas and baking soda and cover the chickpeas with the lukewarm water. Bring the mixture to a gentle boil, and boil the chickpeas for 12 to 15 minutes, or until the chickpeas are soft. Drain the cooking liquid and rinse off the chickpeas with cold water. Transfer the chickpeas to a food processor and allow them to cool for 5 minutes.

Add the tahini, garlic, lemon juice, lemon zest, cumin, ¾ teaspoon of the salt and 4 tablespoons (60 ml) of the oil. Process the ingredients until they are smooth and creamy. Add the ice water, 1 tablespoon (15 ml) at a time, until the hummus reaches your desired consistency.

Place the naan on a medium baking sheet and drizzle the naan with the remaining 1 tablespoon (15 ml) of oil, the remaining ½ teaspoon of salt and za'atar. Bake the naan for 5 to 6 minutes, or until it is warm and slightly toasted. Cut the naan into triangles.

Garnish the hummus with a drizzle of olive oil and a dash of za'atar and serve with the toasted naan, carrots, radishes and cucumber.

STRAWBERRY-BANANA NICE CREAM

This four-ingredient ice cream recipe is a true testament to the beauty of fruit. Made with only ripe frozen bananas and strawberries, a bit of dairy-free milk and a splash of vanilla, this ice cream is the perfect, all-natural, sugar-free treat. The frozen bananas blend to create a luscious, soft-serve base. The strawberries add beautiful berry flavor and vibrant color. Finally, the touch of vanilla helps add a little extra pure natural sweetness. This ice cream is truly magic: no dairy, added sugar or heavy custard base—just a few, simple ingredients to create pure bliss! It's called nice cream because it's ice cream that is truly nice to your body.

YIELD: 4 SERVINGS

3 medium ripe bananas, coarsely chopped and frozen

½ cup (72 g) ripe strawberries, halved and frozen

1 to 3 tbsp (15 to 45 ml) unsweetened plain almond milk or cashew milk, divided

1 tsp pure vanilla extract

In a food processor, combine the bananas, strawberries, 1 tablespoon (15 ml) of the almond milk and vanilla. Process the ingredients until they are smooth and creamy—this will take several minutes. If the fruit is not blending and creates more of a pebble-like consistency, add the remaining 1 to 2 tablespoons (15 to 30 ml) of almond milk, 1 tablespoon (15 ml) at a time, until the nice cream reaches a soft-serve consistency. Do not add too much milk, or the mixture will be more like a smoothie.

Using an ice cream scoop, divide the nice cream among four bowls or ice cream cones.

Notes: You can freeze any extra ice cream scoops—they will last 1 or 2 weeks in an airtight container in the freezer. I recommend setting the ice cream out of the freezer for about 5 minutes before enjoying it, so that it can soften and reach a soft-serve consistency again.

You can also change up the flavors—try different berries or even add peanut butter or chocolate. Just make sure to add the bananas and flavoring first, then the almond milk, 1 tablespoon (15 ml) at a time, until you reach a soft-serve ice cream consistency.

KEY LIME PIE PARFAITS

I just recently had my first piece of Key lime pie while on a trip to Florida, and I was shocked at how much I loved it. You see, I am a chocolate dessert kind of girl. But that Key lime pie was rich, tangy, sweet and sour with a crumbly graham cracker crust and dollops of cool whipped cream, a combination perfect for the hot, sunny days in Florida. I knew I wanted to re-create this dessert but make it healthier by replacing the heavy sweetened condensed milk. So I made Key lime pie pudding parfaits. The pudding is free of dairy and refined sugar but just as zippy, custardy and sweet as a regular Key lime pie filling. It's paired with a honey graham cracker crust and coconut whipped cream to create the ultimate healthy, dairy-free Key lime pie experience.

YIELD: 4 SERVINGS

Pudding

1 (15-oz [444-ml]) can light coconut milk

3 large egg yolks

½ cup (96 g) allulose or organic granulated sugar

½ tsp salt

1 tbsp (6 g) Key lime zest (see Note)

½ cup (120 ml) fresh Key lime juice (see Note)

½ cup (120 ml) cold unsweetened plain almond milk or cashew milk

¼ cup (36 g) cornstarch

1 tsp pure vanilla extract

Parfaits

5½ honey graham crackers

1 tbsp (12 g) coconut sugar

Pinch of salt

2 tbsp (30 g) ghee, melted

1 cup (60 g) coconut whipped cream

4 thin slices Key lime

To make the pudding, combine the coconut milk, egg yolks, allulose and salt in a medium saucepan over medium heat. Bring the mixture to a gentle boil. Cook the mixture for 3 to 4 minutes, until it is frothy on top and hot to the touch.

In a small bowl, combine the lime zest, lime juice, almond milk, cornstarch and vanilla. Mix the ingredients until no lumps are present.

Once the coconut milk mixture is hot, slowly whisk in the almond milk mixture, stirring constantly. Increase the heat to medium-high, and whisk constantly for 5 to 8 minutes, until the pudding thickens. Once the pudding is thick enough to coat the back of a spoon, remove it from the heat.

Transfer the pudding to a large glass bowl. Immediately cover the top of the pudding with plastic wrap, so that the plastic wrap touches the pudding; this will help prevent a "skin" from forming on top of the pudding. Place the bowl in the refrigerator and allow the pudding to set up for at least 4 hours or up to overnight.

Once the pudding is set, make the parfaits. In a food processer, pulse the graham crackers until they resemble sand. Transfer the graham cracker crumbs to a large bowl and stir in the coconut sugar and salt. Add the ghee and stir to combine until the mixture resembles wet sand. Add the graham cracker crust to four small jars, reserving about 1 tablespoon (6 g) of the crust for topping the parfaits. Press down on the crusts to pack them into the jars.

Divide the pudding among the jars on top of the crust. Top the pudding with the coconut whipped cream, reserved graham cracker crumbs and a slice of Key lime.

Note: Sometimes Key limes can be hard to find. If you don't have access to them, run-of-the-mill limes work too!

REFINED SUGAR-FREE EATS
and TREATS

The Swap: Unrefined, natural sugars instead of refined, nutrient-void sugars.

. . . .

I have a mean sweet tooth. I need a little something sweet after every savory meal. I'm a cupcake aficionado and ice cream fanatic. Giving up treats is just not an option in my book. Let's be honest: Cookies and cakes are what makes life, well, a little bit sweeter. So this chapter is dedicated to showing you how to make your favorite treats—and some savory dishes too—healthier by using the right unrefined sweeteners.

It's important to watch your intake of white sugars, including unrefined brown sugar and powdered sugar. These sugars are extremely processed and stripped of their nutrients. They are full of "empty carbs" and many harmful chemicals, including phosphoric acid, bleaching agents, sulfur dioxide and formic acid. Additionally, these sugars can have some negative health effects, such as increased blood sugar and a higher risk of heart disease and diabetes.

Processed sugar is present in more foods than you may realize, not just the obvious things like cookies and cakes. It also makes an appearance in some unsuspected foods, like ketchup, barbecue sauce, pickles, white flour and others. When I select condiments, I always check the ingredient label to select ones with a lower sugar content—the amount of refined sugar in traditional versions of these sweet and savory foods can be alarming!

There is a solution besides saying bye-bye to your beloved baked goods and condiments. Instead, swap out the processed white sugar for natural, unrefined sweeteners. Unrefined sugars contain minerals and nutrients that are stripped from refined sugars. Today, there are a variety of great alternatives you can easily

find in stores. Some of my favorites that you will find in this cookbook are honey, agave, maple syrup, date sugar, fruit, allulose and molasses.

These unrefined sweeteners provide more nutrition for our bodies than processed sugar, which means they are all-natural and easier for the body to digest and process. Of course, as with anything else, they should be enjoyed in moderation. But you can feel better about indulging in your favorite treats knowing the sweeteners have added some nutritional benefits, unlike most refined sweeteners.

I also prefer unrefined sugars because they each have a more robust, unique flavor profile. White sugar tends to add just pure sweetness. Alternatively, sweeteners like honey add a beautiful floral note, while molasses, maple syrup and date syrup add a rich, caramel-like sweetness and agave adds a fruity sweetness. Plus, sweeteners like honey and maple syrup actually have a sweeter taste, so you can use less of them than you would traditional sugars.

In this chapter, you will find delicious desserts like Grandma's Texas Sheet Cake (page 146) and Brown Butter and Coconut Sugar Chocolate Chip Cookies (page 145). You'll also create amazing breakfasts treats like Toasted Coconut and Peanut Butter Granola Bars (page 137) and Strawberry Cheesecake Overnight Oat Parfaits (page 142). You'll even discover some savory dishes like Honey-Garlic Sesame Chicken (page 132), Honey-Dijon and Pecan Baked Salmon (page 141) and my homemade barbecue sauce affectionately dubbed by my husband as Dani's Famous Barbecue Sauce (page 135). Each recipe uses a natural sweetener to provide that sweet taste you desire without all the processed, unwanted ingredients!

HONEY-GARLIC SESAME CHICKEN

Did you know that many classic Chinese takeout dishes are full of white sugar? That's why I decided to give this Honey-Garlic Sesame Chicken a healthy makeover. It still has that sweet and salty umami kick that Chinese food is known for but with half the sugar. The sauce is made with soy sauce, low-sugar sweet chili sauce, sesame oil, fresh orange juice and unrefined honey. All of these ingredients create the perfect balance of salty, sweet and sticky goodness that makes this lightly fried chicken dish just as addictive as takeout, but much more nutritious!

YIELD: 4 TO 6 SERVINGS

Chicken

2 tbsp (18 g) cornstarch

¾ cup (90 g) white whole-wheat flour

1½ tsp (8 g) plus pinch of salt, divided

½ tsp black pepper

1 tsp garlic powder

¼ tsp paprika

2 large eggs, lightly beaten

1½ lb (680 g) boneless, skinless chicken breasts, cut into bite-sized pieces

½ cup (120 ml) avocado oil

Sauce

1 tbsp (15 ml) toasted sesame oil

3 cloves garlic, minced

1 tbsp (15 ml) rice wine vinegar

¼ cup (60 ml) honey

2 tbsp (30 ml) sweet chili sauce (such as Sky Valley brand)

¼ cup (60 ml) soy sauce

Juice of ½ small navel orange

1 tbsp (6 g) orange zest

Pinch of salt

1½ tsp (5 g) cornstarch

2 tsp (10 ml) cold water

For Serving

1 tbsp (9 g) sesame seeds

1 cup (195 g) cooked brown rice

To make the chicken, place the cornstarch in a large ziplock bag. In another large ziplock bag, combine the flour, 1½ teaspoons (8 g) of the salt, black pepper, garlic powder and paprika. Shake the bag until all of the ingredients are well combined. Place the eggs in a large, wide bowl. Set a large baking sheet next to this breading station.

Add the chicken to the bag of cornstarch and shake the bag, so that all of the chicken pieces are coated in cornstarch.

Add the chicken, a few pieces at a time, to the eggs. Ensure that the chicken pieces are well coated in the egg wash.

Add the chicken to the bag of flour and shake the bag, so that all of the chicken pieces are well coated. Shake off any excess flour from the chicken pieces. Transfer the chicken to the baking sheet and allow the chicken to rest for 10 minutes, so that the flour can properly adhere to the meat.

In a large wok or skillet, heat the avocado oil to 375°F (191°C). Ensure that the oil covers the entire bottom of the wok.

Add the chicken to the hot oil in small batches, so as to not overcrowd the wok. Fry the chicken for 3 to 4 minutes per side, or until it is golden brown and crispy and its internal temperature reaches 165°F (74°C). Transfer the chicken to a layer of paper towels to drain. Continue this process until all of the chicken is cooked. Season the chicken with the remaining pinch of salt.

To make the sauce, wipe the wok clean and set it over medium heat. Add the sesame oil, garlic, vinegar, honey, sweet chili sauce, soy sauce, orange juice, orange zest and salt. Cook the sauce for 2 to 4 minutes, until it starts to bubble slightly.

In a small bowl, combine the cornstarch and water, whisking so that no lumps are present. Add the cornstarch slurry to the sauce. Bring the sauce to a gentle boil and cook it for 2 to 3 minutes, stirring constantly, until it has thickened slightly. Add the cooked chicken to the sauce and toss to coat it in the sauce.

Garnish the chicken with the sesame seeds. Serve the chicken over the rice.

BARBECUE CHICKEN BOWLS WITH HOMEMADE BARBECUE SAUCE

These bowls might be my hubby's favorite recipe in this cookbook! The bowl is filled with grilled chicken slathered in my sweet and smoky homemade barbecue sauce, grilled corn, hearty black beans, creamy avocado, salty cotija cheese, bright and juicy cherry tomatoes, crunchy tortilla chips and zesty fresh cilantro. I make my barbecue sauce from scratch, because doing so allows me to make it with fresh, real ingredients and control the amount of sugar. It's shocking the amount of sugar in some store-bought sauces—sometimes more than our daily recommended intake in one small serving. That's why I prefer to make it at home. It's easy and just as delicious! I use date syrup, which has a sweet, molasses-like flavor that works beautifully in barbecue sauce. When the date syrup is combined with a little coconut sugar, real molasses and tons of bold spices, the result is a well-balanced, perfectly sweetened, sticky, delicious barbecue sauce. My hubby gave this sauce a big thumbs-up, naming it Dani's Famous Barbecue Sauce!

YIELD: 4 SERVINGS

Dani's Famous Barbecue Sauce

2 tsp (6 g) smoked paprika

1 tsp onion powder

2 tsp (6 g) garlic powder

½ tsp mustard powder

¼ tsp paprika

¼ tsp cayenne pepper

¼ cup (60 g) tomato paste

1 (15-oz [444-ml]) can tomato sauce

¼ cup (60 ml) date syrup or honey

3 tbsp (36 g) coconut sugar

⅓ cup (80 ml) apple cider vinegar

2 tbsp (30 ml) Worcestershire sauce

1 tbsp (15 ml) molasses

¾ tsp salt

To make Dani's Famous Barbecue Sauce, combine the smoked paprika, onion powder, garlic powder, mustard powder, paprika, cayenne pepper, tomato paste, tomato sauce, date syrup, sugar, vinegar, Worcestershire sauce, molasses and salt in a medium saucepan over medium-high heat. Bring the sauce to a gentle boil, then reduce the heat to medium-low and simmer the sauce for 15 to 20 minutes, until it has thickened slightly. Remove the sauce from the heat. Use the sauce immediately or store it in an airtight container in the refrigerator for up to 2 weeks.

(Continued)

Chicken and Bowls

1 lb (454 g) boneless, skinless chicken breasts

1½ tsp (8 g) salt, divided

½ tsp black pepper

4 medium ears corn, husked

1 tbsp (15 ml) melted butter

2 cups (94 g) coarsely chopped romaine or Bibb lettuce

2 cups (390 g) cooked brown rice

1 (15-oz [425-g]) can black beans, drained and rinsed

1 large avocado, thinly sliced

½ cup (88 g) halved cherry tomatoes

½ cup (32 g) crushed tortilla chips

½ cup (75 g) crumbled cotija cheese

Thirty minutes prior to grilling the chicken, remove it from the refrigerator and allow it to set out at room temperature.

To make the chicken and bowls, preheat the grill to medium heat.

Season the chicken with 1 teaspoon of the salt and the black pepper.

Slather the ears of corn with the butter. Add the corn to the grill. Cook the corn for 3 to 4 minutes per side, turning the ears every minute or so, until all sides of the corn are slightly charred. Remove the corn from the heat and sprinkle the ears with the remaining ½ teaspoon of salt. Cut the kernels off the cobs.

Add the chicken to the grill. Cook the chicken for 4 minutes on the first side. Flip the chicken and brush the opposite side with ¼ cup (60 ml) of the sauce. Cook the chicken for 4 minutes. Flip the chicken again and brush it with another ¼ cup (60 ml) of the sauce. Cook the chicken about 1 minute per side, so that the sauce can caramelize on both sides. When the chicken's internal temperature reaches 165°F (74°C), remove it from the heat and allow it to rest for 5 minutes. Cut the chicken into bite-sized pieces.

Divide the chicken, corn, lettuce, rice, black beans, avocado, cherry tomatoes, tortilla chips and cotija cheese among four wide bowls. Drizzle each serving with additional sauce.

TOASTED COCONUT AND PEANUT BUTTER GRANOLA BARS

Granola bars are an energy-boosting snack. The problem is that store-bought bars can be chock-full of sugar and processed ingredients. Making your own is easy and allows you to control the ingredients, especially the sugar. These Toasted Coconut and Peanut Butter Granola Bars are refined sugar–free and made with protein-rich and wholesome ingredients. The bars are sweetened with dates and a touch of honey. The other star ingredients include peanut butter, walnuts, pecans, oats and chia seeds. Together they create a delicious, nutrient-rich snack you can feel good about eating and giving to your kids!

YIELD: 8 TO 10 BARS

10 to 12 pitted dates

½ cup (61 g) pecans

½ cup (61 g) walnuts

1 cup (76 g) unsweetened shredded coconut

1¼ cups (100 g) rolled oats

1 tsp ground cinnamon

½ tsp salt

½ cup (130 g) creamy or chunky peanut butter

2 tbsp (30 ml) honey

3 tbsp (45 g) plus 1 tsp coconut oil, divided

1 tsp pure vanilla extract

1 tbsp (9 g) chia seeds

½ cup (90 g) dark chocolate chips

In a medium bowl, cover the dates with very hot water. Let the dates sit for 1 hour. This allows the dates to soften, so that they will blend better. Drain the water and gently pat the dates dry. Set them aside.

Line an 8 x 8-inch (20 x 20–cm) baking pan with parchment paper and spray the parchment paper with cooking spray.

Preheat the oven to 325°F (163°C). Lightly grease a large baking sheet.

Spread out the pecans, walnuts and shredded coconut on the prepared baking sheet. Bake the mixture for 5 to 6 minutes, stirring the ingredients after every minute, until the nuts and coconut are toasted. Let the mixture cool slightly.

Place the dates in a food processor. Process until the dates are broken down into chunks. Add the pecans, walnuts, coconut, oats, cinnamon and salt and process until all of the ingredients are well combined and the nuts and oats are broken down. If necessary, use a spatula to scrape the sides of the processor's bowl, then continue to process until the ingredients are well combined.

In a large microwave-safe bowl, combine the peanut butter, honey and 3 tablespoons (45 g) of the oil. Microwave the mixture for about 1 minute, stirring halfway through, until the peanut butter and coconut oil are melted and smooth. Stir in the vanilla.

Add the date-oat mixture to the peanut butter mixture and stir until all of the ingredients are well combined. Fold in the chia seeds.

(Continued)

TOASTED COCONUT AND PEANUT BUTTER GRANOLA BARS (CONTINUED)

Pour the granola mixture into the prepared baking pan and press the mixture down evenly in the pan.

Place the granola mixture in the refrigerator and allow it to set up for at least 2 hours.

Remove the granola from the baking pan and cut it into 8 to 10 bars.

In a small microwave-safe bowl, combine the chocolate chips and the remaining 1 teaspoon of oil. Microwave the mixture at 50 percent power in increments of 45 seconds, until the chocolate and oil are fully melted and smooth.

Pour the melted chocolate into a small ziplock or piping bag. Cut off the corner or tip of the bag, and drizzle chocolate on each granola bar. Allow the chocolate to harden for about 1 hour before serving the granola bars.

Note: Store these bars in an airtight container in the fridge for up to 2 weeks.

Extra Swap: I use real nuts and oats in place of sugary, starchy cereal to make this a gluten-free and protein-packed snack.

HONEY-DIJON AND PECAN BAKED SALMON

This is a flavorful, quick and easy weeknight dinner the whole family will love! Salmon is covered in a honey-Dijon glaze, coated in a pecan crumble and baked to perfection. The problem with so many glazes and sauces is that they are full of unwanted white sugar. But this recipe uses only honey, which provides the perfect amount of rich sweetness without overdoing it. The honey works with the tangy Dijon mustard and pecans to create a delicious, balanced meal.

YIELD: 4 SERVINGS

2 tbsp (30 g) Dijon mustard

2 tbsp (30 ml) honey

2½ tbsp (38 ml) extra virgin olive oil, divided

4 (4-oz [112-g]) skinless salmon fillets

⅓ cup (40 g) Italian breadcrumbs

½ cup (61 g) finely chopped pecans

1 tsp garlic salt

1 tbsp (3 g) finely chopped fresh parsley

Preheat the oven to 425°F (218°C). Grease a medium baking dish.

In a small bowl, mix together the mustard, honey and 1 tablespoon (15 ml) of the oil. Place the salmon fillets in the prepared baking dish, then brush the mustard mixture over the salmon.

In a medium bowl, combine the breadcrumbs, pecans, garlic salt and the remaining 1½ tablespoons (23 ml) of oil. Sprinkle this mixture evenly on top of the salmon fillets in the baking dish.

Bake the salmon for 10 to 12 minutes, or until the topping is golden brown. Allow the salmon to rest for 5 minutes. Garnish it with the parsley and serve.

STRAWBERRY CHEESECAKE OVERNIGHT OAT PARFAITS

These strawberry cheesecake overnight oats are by far the best overnight oats I've ever made, and they're even better in parfaits! The parfaits have all the flavors of a creamy, decadent piece of cheesecake layered with a bright, perfectly sweet and quick-to-make strawberry jam. Best yet, these parfaits are sweetened only with honey and a little stevia. The honey's rich, floral sweetness pairs perfectly with the strawberries. And I love stevia because it's a natural, plant-based, zero-calorie sweetener. The honey and stevia add the perfect amount of sweetness to these oats, making them a delicious, healthy, nutrient-packed breakfast that you can enjoy on the go.

YIELD: 3 TO 4 SERVINGS

Quick Strawberry Jam

1 cup (166 g) coarsely chopped strawberries

2 tbsp (30 ml) honey

2 tbsp (30 ml) fresh lemon juice

Pinch of salt

Strawberry Cheesecake Overnight Oat Parfaits

2½ tbsp (38 g) whipped cream cheese, at room temperature

2 tsp (10 g) vanilla bean paste or 2 tsp (10 ml) pure vanilla extract

1 tbsp (15 ml) honey

1¼ cups (300 ml) unsweetened plain almond milk or cashew milk, divided

1¼ cups (100 g) rolled oats

2 tsp (8 g) stevia-based or monk fruit–based sweetener (such as Whole Earth Sweetener brand)

Pinch of salt

1½ tsp (5 g) chia seeds (optional)

½ cup (83 g) thinly sliced strawberries

¼ cup (20 g) Maple-Nut Granola (page 149)

To make the quick strawberry jam, combine the strawberries, honey, lemon juice and salt in a medium saucepan over medium heat. Bring the mixture to a gentle boil and cook it for 10 to 12 minutes, stirring constantly and mashing the strawberries as they soften, until the jam thickens. Remove the jam from the heat and allow it to cool completely. Transfer it to an airtight container and store it in the refrigerator overnight. The jam will continue to thicken overnight.

To make the strawberry cheesecake overnight oat parfaits, mix together the cream cheese, vanilla bean paste and honey in a large bowl. Slowly add 1 cup (240 ml) of the almond milk, whisking constantly, until the mixture is smooth and creamy.

Add the oats, stevia, salt and chia seeds (if using). Stir the ingredients until they are well combined. Place the oats in the refrigerator to set overnight.

In the morning, take the oats out of the refrigerator and stir them. If they are too thick for your liking, add the remaining ¼ cup (60 ml) of almond milk.

To make the parfaits, place some of the overnight oats in the bottoms of three to four parfait glasses. Place some of the jam on top of the oats to create the middle layer of the parfaits. Finally, top the jam with more overnight oats. Garnish the parfaits with the strawberries and granola.

BROWN BUTTER AND COCONUT SUGAR CHOCOLATE CHIP COOKIES

These Brown Butter and Coconut Sugar Chocolate Chip Cookies are magic! Browning the butter gives it a magnificent nutty taste that makes these cookies extra delicious. The cookies are sweetened with only coconut sugar and a little maple syrup, which makes them delicately sweet and gives them a rich, molasses-like taste that pairs perfectly with the browned butter. To round out these cookies, there is a touch of cinnamon, loads of melty dark chocolate chunks and a little sprinkle of salt at the end.

YIELD: 10 COOKIES

1¼ cups (170 g) all-purpose gluten-free flour blend or 1¼ cups (156 g) all-purpose flour (such as King Arthur Baking or Bob's Red Mill brands)

½ tsp baking soda

½ tsp salt

½ cup (120 g) butter

¾ cup (144 g) coconut sugar

2 tbsp (30 ml) pure maple syrup

2 tsp (10 ml) pure vanilla extract

1 large egg

¾ cup (135 g) dark chocolate chunks

In a large bowl, whisk together the flour, baking soda and salt. Set the flour mixture aside.

In a small saucepan over medium heat, melt the butter. Brown the butter for 8 to 10 minutes, swirling and gently stirring it, until the butter foams, starts to turn brown and smells nutty. Transfer the brown butter to a large bowl. Allow it to cool completely.

Once the butter has cooled, whisk in the sugar, maple syrup and vanilla. Mix the ingredients together until no lumps remain. Whisk in the egg until the mixture is smooth, glossy, pale in color and slightly thickened.

Gently fold in the flour mixture until no dry spots remain. Fold in the chocolate chunks.

Place the cookie dough in the refrigerator for at least 30 minutes to chill.

When you're ready to bake the cookies, preheat the oven to 350°F (177°C). Line a large rimmed baking sheet with parchment paper.

Use a 1½-tablespoon (23-g) cookie scoop to form the dough into 10 balls. Place the cookies on the prepared baking sheet, leaving plenty of space between each cookie.

Bake the cookies for 8 to 10 minutes, until they are golden brown and firm around the edges. Remove the cookies from the oven and bang the baking sheet against a heatproof work surface; this helps create a couple of ripples in the cookies and slightly flatten the cookies. Let the cookies cool slightly on the baking sheet before serving.

Extra Swap: I use a gluten-free flour blend, which combines multiple gluten-free flours that closely mimic regular all-purpose flour. So there is an option to make these cookies both refined sugar–free and gluten-free, making them easier on digestion. I also use dark chocolate, which is high in antioxidants and lower in sugar than milk chocolate.

Note: Gluten-free cookies dry out faster, so they last only about a day at room temperature, so I recommend baking and eating them the same day and freezing extra cookie dough.

GRANDMA'S TEXAS SHEET CAKE

Texas sheet cake has a special place in my heart. It was my grandma's signature dessert that she brought to every family get-together. After she passed, my mom gave me her recipe box, and I found her recipe for this cake. I knew I had to lighten it up with some simple swaps and add it to this cookbook! I was able to do it justice and not sacrifice flavor by replacing the white sugar with allulose. Allulose is a type of sugar that resembles fructose, the sugar that occurs naturally in fruit. It's a great alternative to white processed sugar because it's a natural zero-calorie sweetener that looks like sugar, tastes like sugar and measures like sugar. Like this cake, allulose is pure magic and my new go-to sugar substitute! I know my grandma would approve of my makeover to this cake!

YIELD: 1 (11 X 16-INCH [28 X 41-CM]) SHEET CAKE

Cake

1 cup (240 ml) water

½ cup (120 g) butter

⅓ cup (32 g) unsweetened cocoa powder

½ cup (120 g) coconut oil

2 large eggs, at room temperature

¾ cup (214 g) full-fat plain Greek yogurt, at room temperature

1 tsp pure vanilla extract

1 cup (90 g) oat flour

1 cup (130 g) white whole-wheat flour or 1 cup (120 g) whole-wheat pastry flour

1½ cups (288 g) allulose

1 tsp baking soda

½ tsp salt

Frosting

6 tbsp (90 g) butter

2 tbsp (30 g) coconut oil

5 tbsp (30 g) unsweetened cocoa powder

5 tbsp (75 ml) unsweetened plain almond milk or cashew milk

1 tsp pure vanilla extract

Pinch of salt

3½ cups (420 g) powdered sugar, sifted

To make the cake, preheat the oven to 350°F (177°C). Grease an 11 x 16-inch (28 x 41-cm) jelly roll pan.

In a medium saucepan over medium heat, combine the water, butter, cocoa powder and oil. Bring the mixture to a gentle boil and cook it for 3 to 5 minutes, whisking constantly, until all of the ingredients are well incorporated. Remove the saucepan from the heat and allow the mixture to cool slightly.

In a large bowl, whisk together the eggs, yogurt and vanilla.

In another large bowl, whisk together the oat flour, white whole-wheat flour, allulose, baking soda and salt. Add the yogurt mixture and stir a few times, so that the ingredients are mostly combined. Pour in the chocolate mixture and gently whisk until a smooth batter forms. Pour the batter into the prepared jelly roll pan. Bake the cake for 18 to 20 minutes, or until a toothpick inserted into the center comes out clean.

Allow the cake to cool slightly.

During the final 5 minutes of baking time, make the frosting. Combine the butter, oil, cocoa powder, almond milk, vanilla and salt in a medium saucepan over medium heat. Allow the butter and oil to melt and incorporate with the other ingredients. Bring the mixture to a low boil, then immediately remove it from the heat. Add the powdered sugar and stir until it is well combined with the butter mixture. Pour the frosting over the warm cake, spreading it out evenly so that it covers the whole cake.

Allow the cake to cool completely and the frosting to set before cutting the cake into squares.

Extra Swaps: I use whole-wheat pastry flour and oat flour instead of starchy white flour and protein-packed Greek yogurt and nutrient-rich coconut oil in place of the refined oil and some of the butter.

MAPLE-NUT GRANOLA

I love granola! Paired with vanilla yogurt and berries, it's my go-to breakfast. Granola is often considered a healthy snack, and it certainly can be. But most store-bought kinds are full of sugar and unwanted ingredients. This homemade Maple-Nut Granola is made with real, superfood ingredients, like oats, nuts, sunflower seeds, hemp seeds and coconut oil. Plus, it's sweetened with only real maple syrup and coconut sugar, both unrefined, natural sugars. It's not only good for you but it also tastes amazing. It has a light, crunchy texture and a perfectly sweet, rich, maple-forward flavor. It's my new favorite granola, and I make it almost every week.

YIELD: 10 TO 12 SERVINGS

⅓ cup (80 g) coconut oil

¼ cup (60 ml) pure maple syrup

1 tbsp (15 ml) pure vanilla extract

½ tsp maple extract (see Note)

2 cups (160 g) rolled oats

1¼ cups (151 g) coarsely chopped walnuts, almonds or pecans

½ cup (64 g) roasted unsalted sunflower seeds

¼ cup (40 g) hemp seeds

½ cup (60 g) unsweetened coconut flakes

1 tsp ground cinnamon

3 tbsp (36 g) coconut sugar

½ tsp salt

Preheat the oven to 300°F (149°C). Line a large baking sheet with parchment paper.

In a large microwave-safe bowl, combine the oil and maple syrup. Microwave the mixture for about 1 minute, until the oil is melted. Stir in the vanilla and maple extract.

Add the oats, walnuts, sunflower seeds, hemp seeds, coconut flakes, cinnamon, sugar and salt. Stir the ingredients until everything is well combined. Pour the granola onto the prepared baking sheet and spread it out into a thin, even layer. Bake the granola for 25 to 30 minutes, or until it starts to slightly brown.

Let the granola cool entirely. It will get crunchy as it cools. Break it up into bite-sized pieces. Serve the granola with milk, use it as a topping or serve it on its own.

Note: The maple extract amps up the maple flavor.

Extra Swap: The granola is gluten-free and packed with fiber and protein, because it's made with oats, nuts and seeds instead of processed cereals.

BRIGHT *and* LIGHT LIBATIONS

The Swap: Fresh, real ingredients instead of processed, high-sugar ingredients.

....

Even when I'm trying to eat clean and healthy, I still like to enjoy a good cocktail—or two! Cocktails are often made with processed fruit juices and tons of sugar, which makes them overly indulgent and, in my opinion, unappealing. But this chapter will show you how to make delicious, refreshing and complex cocktails without all the unwanted ingredients. Instead, they are made with unrefined sugars, fresh fruit juices and recognizable ingredients. In these pages, you will find recipes such as my Honey-Raspberry Mojito (page 156), which is made without simple syrup but fresh, ripe berries and floral, natural honey. Then there's my Bourbon-Maple

Hot Chocolate (page 160), made with unprocessed, dark chocolate and almond milk instead of heavy cream. If you're in the mood for something fruity, both the Frozen Piña Colada (page 159) and the Grapefruit Margarita (page 152) are made with fresh fruit and fruit juices instead of sugar-filled, fake mixes. Finally, a bright, fruity and perfectly sweet Citrus Rosé Sangria (page 155) is brimming with fresh juice and natural sweeteners. These healthy, balanced renditions of classic cocktails will have you asking, "Is it five o'clock yet?"

GRAPEFRUIT MARGARITA

Margaritas are one of my favorite cocktails. Unfortunately, they are notorious for being chock-full of sugar and sometimes artificial ingredients. The good news is that margaritas are easy to make at home with real ingredients and less sugar while still being bright and refreshing. This grapefruit margarita combines fresh grapefruit juice, a touch of fruity agave, the perfect amount of tequila and tart lime to create a delicious, crisp cocktail.

YIELD: 2 SERVINGS

3 lime wedges, divided

1 tbsp (15 g) coarse salt

Ice, as needed

⅔ cup (160 ml) fresh grapefruit juice

¼ cup (60 ml) fresh lime juice

3 oz (88 ml) tequila

1½ oz (44 ml) triple sec

2 tsp (10 ml) agave

2 thin slices grapefruit

Use 1 of the lime wedges to wet the rims of two lowball glasses. Pour the coarse salt into a wide mouth bowl and press the rims of the glasses in the salt, so that the tops of the glasses are rimmed with the salt. Fill the glasses with ice.

In a shaker, combine the grapefruit juice, lime juice, tequila, triple sec, agave and additional ice. Shake the mixture vigorously. Strain the margarita into the prepared glasses.

Garnish the margaritas with the grapefruit slices and the remaining 2 lime wedges.

CITRUS ROSÉ SANGRIA

This light, refreshing and perfectly sweet Citrus Rosé Sangria is perfect for warm, sunny days. The beauty of sangria is that it's a make-ahead cocktail that serves a large crowd. In my opinion, sangria tends to be too sweet and overpowered by processed fruit juice. This sangria still allows the rosé wine to shine while being complemented by all-natural fresh citrus fruit juice, a touch of agave and elderflower and orange liqueurs. Finally, it's topped with a little sparkling wine for that fizzy effect to make it truly special. It's a delicious, balanced cocktail that tastes like summertime in a glass!

YIELD: 8 TO 10 SERVINGS

1 small navel orange, thinly sliced

½ small grapefruit, thinly sliced

½ cup (72 g) strawberries, halved

1 (25-oz [739-ml]) bottle rosé wine

1 cup (240 ml) fresh grapefruit juice

½ cup (120 ml) fresh orange juice

2 tbsp (30 ml) agave

½ cup (120 ml) elderflower liqueur

¼ cup (60 ml) orange liqueur

1 cup (240 ml) dry sparkling wine or club soda

In a large pitcher, combine the orange slices, grapefruit slices, strawberries, rosé, grapefruit juice, orange juice, agave, elderflower liqueur and orange liqueur. Stir until the ingredients are well combined. Top the sangria with the sparkling wine.

Note: If you are not serving the sangria the same day, I recommend adding the sparkling wine to each individual glass instead of the pitcher, so that the sangria keeps better. When you're ready to serve, pour the sangria into each individual glass until it is three-quarters full. Top each serving with 2 to 3 tablespoons (30 to 45 ml) of the sparkling wine. Without the sparkling wine, the sangria keeps in the refrigerator for 3 to 4 days.

HONEY-RASPBERRY MOJITO

Mojitos are another one of my favorite cocktails—this one is light, a little bubbly and perfectly flavored with lime and mint. I find that when I get a mojito at a bar or restaurant, it contains too much simple syrup. Simple syrup—which is just a combination of sugar and water—makes the drink cloyingly sweet and less nuanced in flavor. This mojito, on the other hand, is the perfect balance of sweet and tart. It's sweetened with floral, robust honey to provide depth of flavor and ripe raspberries to add a little tartness. This is a delicious, well-balanced and all-natural cocktail you can feel good about sipping on!

YIELD: 1 SERVING

¼ cup (37 g) raspberries, plus more as needed

1 tbsp (15 ml) honey

2 tbsp (30 ml) cold water

2 tbsp (30 ml) fresh lime juice

5 leaves fresh mint, plus more as needed

2 oz (59 ml) white rum

Ice, as needed

About ½ cup (120 ml) club soda

1 lime wedge

In a small bowl, combine the raspberries, honey and water. Muddle the mixture until the raspberries are broken down and release their juices. Strain the mixture into a mixer to remove the raspberry seeds.

Add the lime juice and mint and gently muddle so that the mint releases its flavor. Add the rum and ice and shake the mixture vigorously.

Pour the mojito into a highball glass. Top the mojito with the club soda. Garnish the mojito with additional raspberries, the lime wedge and additional mint.

FROZEN PIÑA COLADA

Anytime I go somewhere tropical for vacation, the first thing I order is a piña colada. It's such a fun, delicious, whimsical drink. Typically, it's filled with tons of sugar and processed coconut cream, making it an only-on-vacation splurge. I created my own version using fresh, real ingredients like fresh pineapple, light coconut milk, freshly squeezed lime and orange juices and a touch of agave, making this an every-weekend-in-the-summer drink!

YIELD: 2 SERVINGS

2 cups (330 g) coarsely chopped fresh, ripe pineapple, frozen

⅓ cup (80 ml) coconut or regular rum

⅔ cup (160 ml) light coconut milk

1 tsp agave

½ tbsp (8 ml) fresh lime juice

1 tbsp (15 ml) fresh orange juice

2 pineapple wedges

2 fresh pitted cherries

In a blender, combine the pineapple, rum, coconut milk, agave, lime juice and orange juice. Blend until the ingredients are smooth.

Transfer the piña colada to two glasses. Garnish each serving with 1 pineapple wedge and 1 cherry.

BOURBON-MAPLE HOT CHOCOLATE

There's nothing better than a warm, boozy cup of hot cocoa on a cold winter's day. Wait—there is! A warm, boozy cup of hot cocoa made with real, natural ingredients that still tastes amazing. This Bourbon-Maple Hot Chocolate is made dairy free with almond milk and quality, low-sugar dark chocolate. It's also sweetened with pure, rich maple syrup. For a kick, there's a little bourbon. This is a delicious, healthy adult hot chocolate.

YIELD: 2 SERVINGS

2 cups (480 ml) unsweetened plain almond milk or light or full-fat coconut milk, divided

1 tbsp (6 g) unsweetened Dutch or regular cocoa powder

3 to 4 tbsp (45 to 60 ml) pure maple syrup

2 to 3 tbsp (30 to 45 ml) bourbon

2 tsp (10 g) vanilla bean paste or 2 tsp (10 ml) pure vanilla extract

½ tsp ground cinnamon

Pinch of salt

⅓ cup (60 g) coarsely chopped dark chocolate

½ cup (30 g) coconut whipped cream (optional)

2 to 4 toasted marshmallows (optional)

In a medium measuring cup, whisk together 1 cup (240 ml) of almond milk, the cocoa powder, maple syrup, bourbon, vanilla bean paste, cinnamon and salt until no lumps are present.

In a small pot over medium heat, combine the remaining 1 cup (240 ml) of the almond milk and the chocolate. Cook the mixture for 2 to 4 minutes, stirring constantly to prevent burning, until the chocolate is fully melted. Pour the bourbon-maple mixture into the hot milk mixture and stir until the two are fully combined. Bring the hot chocolate to a gentle boil and cook it for 3 to 5 minutes, whisking frequently, until it thickens slightly.

Divide the hot chocolate between two mugs, then top each serving with the whipped cream and marshmallows, if using.

ACKNOWLEDGMENTS

At times our own light goes out and is rekindled by a spark from another person. Each of us has cause to think with deep gratitude of those who have lighted the flame within us.

—Albert Schweitzer

To Deano, my loving husband, who always believes in me—even when I don't believe in myself—and pushes me to pursue my dreams. You are my best taste tester, sous chef, dishwasher and hand model, and your support is what made this book possible.

To my parents, thank you for instilling a strong work ethic in me, always fueling my passions, supporting my crazy dream to start a food blog and surprising me with my first professional DSLR camera. I could not have done this without you.

To my brothers, thank you for cheering me on, tasting my food or making my recipes and always reposting and sharing my content. Your unwavering support of my blog and cookbook means the world to me.

To my in-laws, Ann and Dean, and my sister-in-law, Vanessa, thank you so much for always trying my recipes and giving me honest feedback. You helped perfect so many recipes in this book. Also, thank you to the whole Davis crew for your support and love through this process.

To my baby boy, Grayson, my favorite little sous chef and cutest taste tester. Everything I do is for you!

A very special thank-you to all the readers of Danilicious Dishes. Every day I'm blown away that so many of you follow my blog and make my recipes. Your support is what made Danilicious Dishes grow, and it motivates me to keep creating delicious, healthy recipes. This book is for all of you, so that you can keep eating the food you love and feel good about it!

Finally, a huge thank-you to my publisher, Page Street Publishing. I can never thank you enough for seeing the potential in my idea for this cookbook and helping me bring the vision to life. Your team was with me every step of the way to make this book truly special. Thank you!

ABOUT THE AUTHOR

Danielle Davis is the photographer, recipe creator, author and food lover behind the blog Danilicious Dishes. She created the blog to show the world that healthy cooking is anything but boring. The recipes on her blog focus on creative, flavor-forward and nutritious takes on her favorite dishes that are made healthier through clever swaps and nutrient-rich ingredients. These principles have guided and fueled this book.

Danielle is both a health nut and foodie. She believes food is fuel and eating fresh, nutritious food is key to staying energized and happy. She also loves to cook, experiment in the kitchen and, of course, eat delicious food—especially dessert! That is why she is always finding inventive ways to give her favorite dishes a healthy spin.

Danielle also has a passion for writing and art. From a young age, she exercised her creative side and spent her summers in writing and drama classes. As an adult, she pursued her love of writing and received her BA in English with honors from the University of Illinois and a JD, magna cum laude, from Southern Illinois University School of Law. Through her food blog and food photography, she is able to combine her passions of cooking, writing and art.

Danielle lives in Bloomington, Illinois, with her husband, Deano, and their son, Grayson. Her husband is her trusty taste tester and editor. She hopes to instill her love of cooking in Grayson, her mini sous chef.

Danielle has been featured in *Thrive* magazine and *Marketplace* magazine, on ABC's *The Chew* and on popular websites such as feedfeed, Food52 and TODAY Food.

INDEX

....